GW01252088

Scottish Hostels

Scotland's Hostel Directory & Guide 2003/4

Scottish Hostels Ltd

ISBN 0 - 9544750-0-3

Scottish Hostel Guide 2003/4

1st Edition

Layout :   Tim Watson

Design :   Tim Watson

Editorial :   Tina Cuthbertson

British Library Cataloguing in Publication Data
A catalogue record for this book is available from the British Library
ISBN 0 - 9544750-0-3

Published by : Scottish Hostels Ltd
Registered Office:-
1 Achluachrach
By Roy Bridge
Inverness-shire
PH31 4AW
Tel :   01397 712315
Fax :   01397 712013
Email: guide@scottish-hostels.com

Text Copyright © Scottish Hostels Ltd 2003
Photographs Copyright © 2003
Tim Watson, Gavin Hogg, Tina Cuthbertson, Chris Rix.
Printed by : RCS
Cover Artwork :   Tim Watson Ossian International Ltd
Maps & Illustrations :   Felicity Nightingale

Distributed in the UK by :-
Cordee Books and Maps
3a De Montfort Street
Leicester
LE1 7HD
Tel: 0116 2543579
Front cover photograph Suilven, Sutherland

Scottish Hostels Guide 2003/4

Contents

How to use this guide:

Hostels are listed in this booklet in numerical order, on an area basis. To find the entry for a particular hostel from its number on the centre page map, simply use the hostel number as a guide rather than the page numbers. To see information on a particular area and the hostels in that area, use the page number listing above.

Additional Information

The additional information on travel, transport & things to do in each area is designed to highlight some key points – but can never be a fully comprehensive guide to everything in Scotland. Contact individual hostels for a more detailed idea of transport and travel in their immediate area, plus any local events – for example live music, Highland Games, Festivals etc.

There is also much more information on our website:
www.scottish-hostels.com
Plus updated versions of this guide and other essential information – often available for download as PDF files.

Disclaimer

Scottish Hostels Ltd believes that the information given in this guide is correct at the time of going to print. We cannot accept any responsibility for any errors or omissions in the information provided – please always check details with individual hostels if you have any special requirements. If you have any problems do advise us of any mistakes so that they can be corrected in future editions of the Scottish Hostels Guide. Thank you.

Welcome to the Scottish Hostels guide for 2003/4.

The next couple of pages explain a bit about Scottish Hostels -
but for the best experience come and stay at a few!

Why stay in a hostel, bunkhouse or bothy?
If you want to experience an individual type of accommodation, which is unique "one off", flexible, cost effective, informal and friendly, then a hostel is the real answer in the Highlands, Islands & Lowlands of Scotland. It is possible to mix with other like-minded folk as an individual, family or larger group. You will meet independent travellers touring the globe and working en-route, overseas students on a break while studying in the UK, independent outdoor enthusiasts, both from the UK and overseas, and many others – wildlife enthusiasts - walkers – climbers – mountaineers in winter – canoeists – kayaks – skiers – surfing enthusiasts – in fact all sorts of people of all ages from all over the world.

What is a hostel or bunkhouse?
Most hostels cater for travellers and outdoor enthusiasts who are looking for friendly, comfortable, cost effective and flexible accommodation in a convenient location for their travels or to take part in a chosen activity. All hostels – no matter if they are family run, independently owned or part of a network will be highly individual – no two hostels will ever offer the same experience. The owners of hostels are even more unique than the hostel and bunkhouses.
There will mainly be bunk-style sleeping accommodation or on Alpine style sleeping platforms. Many hostels also have twin, double or family rooms. All offer communal facilities to cook your own meals at reasonable times, washing/shower facilities, communal dining / eating areas, and the use of drying room.

Are there any rules?
There is a minimum of rules in all the hostels for your own safety and that of other guests. Please respect these. Access after hours may be limited at individual hostels, but often owners/managers offer a late pass or key with a security deposit. There may be specific check out times on your day of departure – please check with the hostel owner.

Who can use a hostel?
All the hostels listed here are generally open to anyone – individuals, families and groups are welcome. Please check with the hostel owner/manager before booking or arrival if you are a family with young children who may require any special facilities.

A very few Hostels only, accept pre-booked groups – this is clearly shown in their entry – don't turn up at these hostels on chance for a bed.

How do I book?
If possible you should always pre-book direct with the hostel of your choice. It is always worth contacting the hostel in advance to check that there is a free bed – especially in the busy summer months, in remoter areas and during the winter in the ski/winter mountaineering areas. Most hostels will hold a 'same-day' telephone booking to a certain time, but many will require a deposit for advanced bookings, or at least a credit card number.

What does a hostel or bunkhouse provide?
All the Hostels with an enhanced entry in this guide have agreed to operate to a basic set of 'Essential Standards' that ensure the guest can expect satisfactory levels of facilities and cleanliness. The standards will be clearly displayed in all the Hostels, are listed on our website and in this guide.
You can expect to use all hostel facilities, be able to cook your own meals and use washing/toilet facilities – at all reasonable times. All hostels are open to guests already booked in – but there will usually be a check out time on departure day. All hostels will have fully equipped self-catering kitchens suitable for the size/location of the Hostel.

The dining/eating and lounge areas should allow the vast majority of the guests to eat or relax at the same time, and you should find an appropriate number of showers (with hot water) / toilets etc for the size of Hostel. All bedding and freshly laundered bed linen will be provided free of charge or for hire. Many of the hostels listed in the Directory section will also operate to similar standards – but have not signed an agreement to do so – contact these hostels directly to confirm their standards & quality policies.

What do I need to bring with me?

Not a great deal - except for food, which can often be bought in the local area on arrival with the advantage of local produce– or in one of the larger towns en-route which have supermarkets (Oban-Fort William-Inverness-Ullapool-Thurso etc). Ask your hostel owner for information on local shops and their opening hours before you stock up at home. Hostels that only hire bedding may allow you to use your own sleeping bags etc, but those that provide the bedding will ask that you do not use your own. You should always bring a towel, as these are generally not provided. It pays to check with the hostel owner/manager if there is anything else not provided.

Do I have to cook my own meals?

Certainly not! Not all - but some - hostel operators offer an excellent full meal service, breakfast only or a packed lunch service – with good local produce. Others are close to take-aways, or pubs/restaurants that serve a range of meals. Where the hostel provides cooked meals for some guests, there will always be a separate kitchen for the sole use of hostellers wanting to cook their own meals.

Can I get a Group Discount or Exclusive use of a Hostel?

Many visitors to the hostels and bunkhouses participating in this booklet come as part of a group – with families; extended families; friends going away for a social or activity break. Most of the hostels in this booklet will be happy to discuss an exclusive booking for the whole of a bunkhouse or hostel for a period of time – maybe just for a weekend away. Some of the hostels included here only take pre-booked groups. Most – but not all - hostel operators will offer some competitive discounted rates for exclusive bookings where your group would have the sole use of a hostel or bunkhouse unit. Please ask at individual hostels if they offer this facility.

Family Rooms

Family rooms are available in many hostels and bunkhouses – which are ideal for a small group of friends or family group of any age some with inclusive en-suite facilities. There is usually no lower age limit – please ask advice at the hostel of your choice if the facility and hostel type is suitable for your family group.

Where do I get Local Information?

Your very first port of call should be the operator of the hostel you are staying in. They should have copies of local bus/train/ferry timetables at least for visitors plus local taxis and car hire if need be. Some hostels have local detailed maps / local guidebooks for free use or hire to folk staying with them. There may be a full information pack at your hostel of local things to do & places to visit. The local Tourist Information Centre may also be able to help with more information as well as booking longer distance travel tickets. This booklet tries to offer as much local information as possible within a limited space – you will find more detailed information on our web site **www.scottish-hostels.com**

Essential Standards for Hostels & Bunkhouses

All Hostels that have subscribed to marketing options with Scottish Hostels Ltd have agreed to comply with the operating standards given below. You can expect at least these minimum level of standards at any Hostel with a main entry in our guide. This does not apply to hostels only listed in the directory – these hostels may comply with similar standards but you should contact them directly to confirm this.
If for any reason you feel that a particular hostel is not following these standards please take the matter up with the owner or manager of the hostel concerned who should be able to assist you with your concerns.
In the very unlikely event that the owner/manager is unable to resolve any problems please feel free to contact Scottish Hostels directly and we will follow up your concerns with the hostel, and respond directly to you.
Contact Details: Scottish Hostels, c/o Old School, Fiscavaig Rd, Portnalong, Isle of Skye, IV47 8SL.
E-mail: comments@scottish-hostels.com   Web: www.scottish-hostels.com

General
1. The owner, manager and staff should operate a policy of duty of care in all respects to all visitors
2. The hostel should comply with all local authority and fire regulations and the premises must comply with all required statutory requirements.
3. The hostel should be covered by, and should display certification of, full Public Liability Insurance
4. There should be a high standard of general tidiness along with effective maintenance of the hostel and its grounds.
5. There should be a high standard of hygiene and cleanliness throughout.
6. There must be some provision for the safe heating of, at least, the common room.
7. There should be no curfew at night, or a late pass key should be available (deposit acceptable)
8. The hostel should provide accommodation for guests with no minimum period of stay. Where only groups are catered for this should be indicated on hostel promotional literature.
9. Any limitations in the hostel opening hours/ reception/ availability of keys should be indicated on hostel promotional literature and at the time of booking.
10. There shall be adequate capacity and effective provision for the drying of wet clothing and outdoor equipment.

11. Charges
Overnight charges should include full use of self-catering kitchen facilities and kitchen equipment. Where there are limitations on use (eg in the interests of safety/security) this must be clearly stated on hostel promotional literature.
The nightly rates including all extras should be displayed in the hostel reception area. promotional literature, and stated at the time of booking. It must be clearly indicated whether any charge is all inclusive, or what extras might be expected.

12. Kitchen/Dining
a. There should be full self-catering facilities.
b. There should be sufficient crockery and cutlery for the number of bed spaces available
c. There should be a minimum of one cooking ring per 4 guests, with a minimum overall of 4 rings.
d. Where hostels have 24 or less beds there should be sufficient dining places for all guests to sit and eat a meal at the same time. For hostels with more than 24 beds there should be one dining place available for each additional two beds.
e. Where cooked meals are provided to guests a separate full self catering kitchen must be available

13. Toilet/Washroom
a. There should be a minimum of one hot shower for every 12 persons plus a minimum of one toilet & washbasin per 10 persons, in each hostel unit. Where there is a charge for the use of showers or electricity this must be indicated on hostel promotional literature.

14. Sleeping
a. Clean blankets/duvets/bedding should be available free or for hire. Where there is a charge this must be indicated on hostel promotional literature.
b. There shall be one bed/bunkbed available for each designated bedspace advertised.

15. Multi-units and Annexes
a. Where an annexe or other separate sleeping accommodation is used this must be indicated at the time of booking
b. Where there is more than one hostel on one site, each unit shall comply with the standards set out above

FROM COTTAGES TO CASTLES

Top Hostels in top cities
We have great Hostels close
to the hearts of the fun-filled
cities of Edinburgh and Glasgow.
Remember, all our city Hostels
have late opening and the best
facilities including internet
access, plus in summer we
have extra Hostels in Edinburgh
with single rooms.

Spend a night in our haunted
Highland castle, if you dare!
Carbisdale Castle has it's own statue gallery, art collection and
ghost! An unmissible experience on any tour of Scotland.

Escape to Scotland's wild places
Loch Ossian and Glen Affric are
rustic hostels with unique
atmospheres in get-away-from-
it-all settings. Or maybe you
fancy chilling out on one of
our small seaside Hostels?
Imagine empty sandy beaches,
seascapes andsunsets...

Free Overnight at Scottish Youth Hostels! Collect 7 stamps on
your SYHA Reward Card and receive 1 free overnight at any of
our Hostels across Scotland.
(conditions apply)

Booking Is Easy!
Book on line at our secure site:
visit www.syha.org.uk
Our Reservations Team will book
your bed at any SYHA Hostel in
Scotland: call 0870 1 55 32 55 or
e-mail reservations@syha.org.uk
There's no booking fee.

 Scottish Youth Hostels - www.syha.or.uk

Highlands and Islands Travel & Transport.

Travel to the Highlands.

From Overseas – long haul.
There are limited Trans-Atlantic flights into Glasgow, but essentially the majority of travellers from North America & outside Europe will have to pass through London (Gatwick is better than Heathrow as there is a direct link to Inverness), Manchester (also with a direct link to Inverness) or Amsterdam (for connections to Aberdeen).

From elsewhere in Europe.
There are a number of flights direct to Central Scotland from Europe – these include routes from Norway, Amsterdam, Paris & Dublin. The 'traditional' airlines fly into Glasgow, Edinburgh or Aberdeen – details of all these flights are on the BAA website www.baa.com.
Of the newer 'low-cost' airlines Ryanair offers direct flights to Glasgow Prestwick from Paris, Dublin, Brussels, Oslo & Frankfurt. Ryanair also fly from Dublin to Edinburgh & Aberdeen. easyJet offer a low-cost service from Amsterdam to Edinburgh & Glasgow. FlyBE operate to Edinburgh from Paris & Brussels. Direct flights to Aberdeen are offered by KLMuk from Amsterdam, and SAS from Stavanger.
There are no direct flights to Inverness from Europe – apart from specialist charter flights. easyJet fly to London Luton & London Gatwick from many European cites, some well timed to connect with the daily Luton or Gatwick to Inverness easyJet flights. There may be similar connecting flights to Inverness with BA via London Gatwick, Glasgow or Edinburgh. BA have now lowered many prices, and dropped the requirement to stay a Saturday night to obtain their low fares. Connecting flights are also possible from European destinations to Inverness via Manchester with Eastern Airways.
Connecting flights to Glasgow/Edinburgh are possible with Go & Ryanair via London Stanstead, and easyJet via London Luton.

By Ferry
Superfast Ferries now offer a daily direct Ferry service from Zebrugge direct to Rosyth (north of Edinburgh) – ideal if you wish to bring your car & travel independently.

Travel From elsewhere in the UK.

By Air.
Direct flights to Inverness are provided by BA and easyJet from London Gatwick, easyJet from London Luton and Eastern Airways from Manchester.

There are numerous flights from Regional airports in the UK to Edinburgh, Glasgow and Aberdeen – details from www.baa.com. Ryanair have flights from regional UK airports (including Bournemouth & Stanstead) to Glasgow Prestwick. Other low-cost flights to central Scotland (Glasgow/Edinburgh/Prestwick) are available from easyJet (Luton, Stanstead & Gatwick), and FlyBE (Birmingham, London City). FlyBE also fly to Dundee from London City. Eastern Airways fly to Edinburgh from Norwich & Humberside, and Aberdeen from Norwich, East Midlands & Humberside – with onward flight to Wick.

By Road.
Recent improvements have significantly reduced the driving time to the Highlands from much of the UK. Perth – the southern gateway to the Highlands - is about 8 hours driving time from London via the M40, M6, M74 & A9. It helps to have 2 drivers!

Travel From elsewhere in the UK.

By Rail/Coach.
Standard services to Glasgow, Edinburgh & Aberdeen are operated by Virgin Trains or GNER (also to Inverness). The Scotrail sleeper services from London operate to Glasgow, Edinburgh, Aberdeen, Inverness & Ft William. The Inverness sleeper also stops at Dalwinnie, Newtonmore Kingussie & Aviemore – and connects with onward services to Kyle of Lochalsh and Wick/Thurso. The Ft William sleeper stops at all stops north of Glasgow and connects with services to Mallaig. The sleeper train also has a low-cost 1st class seating carriage as well as the tradition sleeping berths. 'Bargain Berth' fares from £19 one way are available only from the Scotrail website. There are also overnight coaches to major cities from London Victoria coach station, operated by Citylink or National Express.

Travel within the Highlands.

By Car.
Despite the high cost of fuel, the independence allowed by having your own transport offers the greatest flexibility for travel within the Highlands. If you have not driven to Scotland, or taken the new ferry direct from Zebrugge you may wish to consider a hire car. The major firms have offices in all the cities and at main airports and train stations. EasyCar offer low cost car rental from Glasgow. Details of local car hire firms are given in the area information sections.

By Train.
All the train services wholly within Scotland are operated by Scotrail – although you can catch GNER or Virgin Train Services on some Inter-City routes where these have started south of the border. Scotrail offer a variety of rover tickets (accepted by Virgin & GNER) that also offer free or discounted ferry travel and are even accepted on some coach services where there are no trains (to Ullapool for example).

By Bike.
Possible the best way to see the Highlands – many of the Highland roads are ideal for cycling (well – apart from the hills!) We have included details of bike repair & bike hire in the local information sections. Be sure to check with rail (free transport on Scotrail), bus & ferry operators on their policy on transporting bikes before you turn up to travel.

By Ferry.
The majority of the ferries to/from the Western Isles are operated by Caledonian MacBrayne (CalMac). Good value discount tickets are available on the Island Hopscotch and the Island Rover tickets, and travel is included on the Scotrail rover tickets. P&O Scottish Ferries operate the main services to Orkney & Shetland (Northlink Ferries from Oct 2002).

By Bus.
InterCity services are operated by Citylink or National Express. The Royal Mail PostBus services serve the rural communities throughout the Highlands. Local firms offering other routes are listed in the local area information pages.

By Air.
In addition to flights to the Islands (detailed in the relevant area pages) Eastern Airways operate a flight from Aberdeen to Wick, and Highland Airways offer an air charter service from their base in Inverness.

Contact Details:

Easyjet	0870 600000	www.easyjet.co.uk
British Airways	08457 733377	www.britishairways.com
Go		www.go-fly.com
British European		www.flybe.com
Ryanair	08457 222222	www.ryanair.com
Eastern Airways	01652 680600	www.easternairways.co.uk
ScotAirways	0870 6060707	www.scotairways.co.uk
BAA		www.baa.co.uk
Inverness Airport	01667 464000	www.hial.co.uk
Super fast Ferries		www.superfastscotland.com
CalMac	01475 650100	www.calmac.co.uk
P&O Ferries	01224 572615	www.poscottishferries.co.uk
Northlink Ferries	01856 851144	www.northlinkferries.co.uk

Perthshire, Southern Cairngorms & Lochnagar

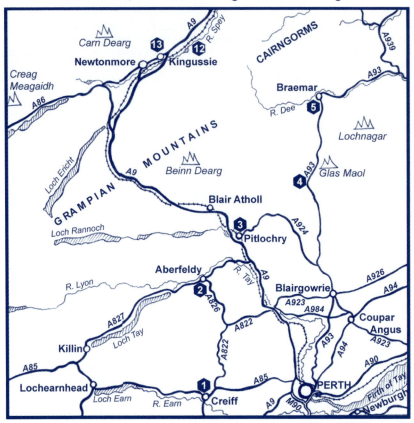

Located in the very heart of Scotland, with the Cairngorm and Grampian Mountains to the north, the central plains of the rivers Forth and Clyde to the south, and the Aberdeenshire coast to the east. Here the air is fresh, the rivers are deep, pure and fast flowing. Here you can walk, ski, sail, climb, kayak & canoe, delve into our history, taste our whisky – and the scenery isn't too bad either.

Pitlochry is situated at the gateway to the Scottish Highlands, surrounded by stunning countryside and mountain scenery and is a colourful and busy Victorian town with the River Tummel running along its edge.

A must is a tour to the Pitlochry Dam and Fish Ladder for a fascinating view of salmon negotiating the specially constructed ladder allowing them to bypass Pitlochry Dam into the man-made Loch Faskally.

No holiday in the Pitlochry area is complete without a visit to 'Scotland's Theatre in the Hills'. The Pitlochry Festival Theatre lies on the banks of the River Tummel and is internationally renowned for its fine repertoire of drama and comedy.

Perthshire Crannog

Loch Tay - at some 14 miles/23 km long this is Perthshire's largest loch. Ancient settlers once lived on Loch Tay, on man-made islands called crannogs. The remains of 18 such islands are still preserved in the loch. These are brought to life at The Scottish Crannog Centre a wonderfully reconstructed crannog built on the loch, painting a fascinating picture of early Iron Age life.

Crieff, Comrie & Strathearn - 'This is where the lowlands meet the highlands'

Strathearn - the broad valley of the River Earn - has been a travel route and resting-place for travellers of all kinds for centuries. Crieff is a small, thriving town on the slopes of the Grampian Mountain foothills. This is where the lush countryside of the Lowlands meets the upland slopes of the Perthshire Highlands.

In the 18th century, **Crieff** was an important cattle trading centre. Cattle drovers, reevers and crofters from the Highlands and Islands would make their long journeys, using now forgotten drove roads through the mountains and hillsides to the north and west, in order to trade livestock at the huge cattle market known as the 'tryst'.

Nearby **Comrie** is an important small village where wild birds are hatched at Auchingarrich Wildlife Centre; earthquakes are housed – Comrie's geological position on the Highland Boundary Fault has caused it to experience many earth tremors and it was here that the world's very first seismometers were set. Loch Earn has excellent facilities for water sports enthusiasts - windsurfers and water-skiers can make the most of unsurpassed facilities and surroundings on Loch Earn.

Further to the north and east the higher arctic Grampian Mountains and Cairngorms, tumbling rivers, 300 Km of coastline, rolling countryside and unique local history make the area an excellent destination for independent travellers, outdoor enthusiasts and families all year round

Walking is probably the main activity for those visiting the area.
The inland eastern slopes of the Cairngorms and the Lochnagar range, is a mecca for hardy walkers and winter mountaineers keen to finish off their Munros – of which there are plenty in this area! Especially accessible from the settlements of Braemar and Glenshee – where there are good hostels to use as a base – all year round.

There are also a wide range of forest trails plus old drove roads through the upland moor and hill areas. Around the spectacular coastline of Aberdeenshire is an extensive network of coastal and countryside walks. It is also now possible to walk the Long Distance Speyside Way from Buckie (and Aviemore), through the Whisky Trails of Morayshire for over 100km, by way of distilleries, old railway tracks and forests. Parts of the route are also open to cyclists or mountain bikes.

Outdoor activity based visits to the area are not limited to walking the extensive hills or climbing the crags of the Aberdeenshire area. Mountain biking tracks, cycling, riding & trekking, sailing and paddlesports are all on offer – either as an independent group – doing your own thing or with one of the many outdoor operators in the area. The winter downhill ski areas of Glen Shee and the Lecht are now excellent year round family and group activity destinations – whether there is snow or not!

Perthshire Travel & Transport Information

Perth is the centre of the Scottish Citylink network, with a service to all of Scotland's cities – the main operators are StageCoach Perth Tel 01738 629339; Strathtay Scottish in Dundee Tel 01382 228345. There are bus/coach links to Pitlochry for access to the A9 south and Inverness to the north. Link to the west coast via a bus route Pitlochry to Rannoch rail station – then by rail to Fort William and the west coast. Crieff/Comrie is acccessible by bus from Aberfeldy, or Perth and St Fillans in Strathearn, or Stirling via Dunblane.

The east Coast and St Andrews can be reached via Kinross. Glen Shee ski and mountain area can be accessed from Blairgowrie.
The main railway routes connect from Glasgow - Stirling - Perth, then from Perth north - Inverness; from Edinburgh - Perth then north - Inverness or east - Aberdeen or Dundee.

All Perthshire Travel Information Guides & maps can be obtained by calling 0845 3011130 Mon-Fri – Local call rates or write to The Public Transport Unit, Perth & Kinross Council, Pullar House, 35 Kinnoull Street Perth, PH1 5GD.

Walking & Climbing in Perthshire the Trossachs, Glen Shee & Braemar areas

Walking is probably the main outdoor activity for those visiting this area. The inland eastern slopes of the Cairngorms, the Perthshire hills and the Lochnagar range is a mecca for hardy walkers and winter mountaineers alike – all keen to finish off their Monros. There are plenty to choose from in this area. These are especially accessible from the settlements around Aberfeldy, Pitlochry, Callander, Braemar and Glenshee – where there are good hostels to use as a base all year round.

Walking leaflets / guides
All available from Perthshire Tourist Board Tel 01738 450600
See the booklet "Hillwalking in Grampian Highland and Aberdeen" from Tourist Information Public Transport Post Bus Services: Serving Aberfoyle, Brig o'Turk, Inversnaid, Strathyre and Lochearnhead. Contact for info Telephone: 01877 330267 or Perth & Kinross Council for the Public Transport Map. To extend walks try the Heather Hopper Bus which normally runs twice-weekly Braemar – Pitlochry, July and August (see time-tables or enquire at the Information Office).

Hill Walk Days.
Ben Ledi - 5- 9 miles – 2800ft – 2-3 hours. Ben Vorlich – Stuc a' Chroin – a good mountain day – start at GR 634233 – OS Sheet 51 and 57 – 4-6 hours – 943m. Ben Venue – 5 miles – 2 cars useful here; Ben Lomond – OS Sheet 56 – about 6 hours – a definite "munro".- stay on the track up the ridge especially in poor visibility.
Ben Lawers - 3984ft start at 1400ft up S slope at car park - 1'1/2 hour nature trail .Whole mountain is a national nature reserve. Serious mountain day on the classic Ptamigan Ridge. OS Sheet 51 – GR 609379 at visitor centre – 5-9 hours. Carnwell Hills, Glen Shee – Start GR 138783 in Glen Shee Car park – OS Sheet 43 – takes 3-5 hours.

Rock Climbing
Largely restricted to Out Crop Climbing & Sport Climbing in the area. Perthshire is one of the main areas for outcrop climbing – varying in height from 8m to 90m - usually low lying and fairly easy to access. Craig a Barns near Dunkeld - schist crags with over hangs and slabs. Glen Lednock crags up to 50 m high. Weem Rock – near Aberfeldy - excellent schist. Glen Ogle – west of Perth - 200 short routes – 7-10m long – close to road. Ben A'an – Loch Achray – exposed short slab routes – good rope lengths. Lochnagar – major, long mountain routes for winter and summer. Broad Cairn – second only to Lochnagar for major rock and winter routes. Glen Clova, Glen Isla, Glen Callater, Glen Doll – a wide variety of standard routes.

Mountain Days
Lochnagar – Royal Deeside above Balmoral Castel. Height 115m OS Map 44 – Ballater, Glen Clova & Surrounding area. Accessible from Ballater, Braemar and Balmoral. A major walking, rock climbing and winter mountaineering / ice climbing mountain area. There is the normal, easier, route from Glen Muick paid car park at GR 310852 - awesome crags Major focus of winter routes. Longer Route via Glen Gelder from near Craithie Church.

Long Distance Walks and Mountain Routes
Rob Roy Way 70 miles / 111 km. Fairly low level distance walk with no great steep or rocky stretches. Starts at Aberfoyle in the National Park, through Menteith Hills, past Falls of Leny to village of Strathyre, follows route of redundant Stirling – Crianlarich rail track, touches Balquidder Glen, up Glen Ogle then turns east to shores of Loch Tay, through Glen Almond, Aberfeldy - finally to Pitlochry. Look also at the Atholl Trail (Perthshire).
Outdoor operators who provide walking, mountaineering and climbing
North West Frontiers - Ullapool based - Scotland wide walking holidays Tel 01854 612628
Free Spirits – Abseiling/Climbing – Aberfeldy. Tel 01887829280
Cairnwell Mountain Sports - Abseiling/Climbing /Guided Walks Tel 01250 885255
Beyond Adventure -
Abseiling/Climbing/Mountaineering/ Hill Walking – Aberfeldy Tel 01887 829202
C-n-Do Scotland – based in Stirling – Tel 01786 445703
Nae Limits – Dunkeld – Mainly Adrenalin sports– Tel 01350 727242
Maps
OS Landranger 1:50,000 OS Outdoor Leisure Maps 1:25,000
No 57: Stirling and The Trossachs Area; No 39: Loch Lomond;
OS Sheets 43, 51, 56. OS Map 44 – Ballater, Glen Clova & Surrounding area.

Cycling & Mountain Biking Perthshire, The Trossachs, Glen Shee & Braemar Area
Forest District Office, Callander Tel 01877 382383
CTC Off-road (national) Colin Palmer. Tel 01531 633500
Selected Cycle Routes in Perthshire – Perthshire Tourist Board Tel 01738 450600
There are endless opportunities for cycling in the Lomond National Park – from Loch Lomond to Callander and Balquidder in the east. - many routes are perfectly straightforward without being too challenging – often through the forests. However there are more adventurous challenging routes on the higher-level forest routes.

Cycle Hire
Trossachs Cycles,	Aberfoyle	Tel 01877 382614
Scottish Cycle Centre,	Callander	Tel 01877 331100
Mounster Bikes,	Callander	Tel 01877 331052
Dunolly Adventure Outdoors,	Aberfeldy	Tel 01887 820298
Highland Adventure Centre,	Glen Isla	Tel 01575 582238
Braemar Mountain Sports,	Braemar	Tel 01224 41242
Cairnwell Mountain Sports,	Glenshee	Tel 01250 885238

Canoesports in the Perthshire, Trossachs & Grampian Areas.

This whole wide area has an extreme diversity of paddling opportunities! So much so that it is difficult to give a concise over view of what is realistically on offer – on inland lochs, extensive long white water rivers, sandy surfing beaches, and a long coastline with some massive cliffs but few islands to explore - always check the weather and the tides locally. The town of Callander has – within 15 miles, 11 inland lochs and 5 main rivers to choose from.

Sea Kayaking - the Aberdeen-shire and Fife coastal areas offer local sea trips to explore the East Coast with its sandy beaches and towering cliffs – but few island hopping opportunities. The Don and Dee Estuaries offer more sheltered water but the tides need to be carefully calculated.

River Kayaking. The east of Scotland is home to some longer, bigger volume rivers than those in the west. The river Tay at Grantully which is the usual site for the Scottish Slalom championships in the autumn.

Inland Lochs. There are also a number of inland lochs of varying size, remoteness and accessibility for various journeys. Some of these can be linked to form much longer journeys - Loch Rannoch, Earn, Tay, Lochay, Tummel and Lomond are the largest stretches of open water and the most popular inland lochs for Open Canadian Canoeing. There are however a number of smaller inland lochs – particularly in the Trossachs area which are accessible for open water canoeing.

Journeying.
Trans-Scotland paddling routes have developed which link up across the main water shed via rivers and inland lochs.

Surf Kayaking. The most popular beaches are in the Aberdeen and St Andrews Bay area – which can produce excellent surf if the wind/tide conditions are right. The tidal estuary conditions require care.

Instruction / river guiding or expeditions. Canoe/kayak hire.

Adventurer's Escape,	Aberfeldy.	Tel 01887 820489
Forest Hills Water Sports,	Loch Ard	Tel 01877 387775
Lochearn Activity Centre,	Lochearn	Tel 01567 830330
Standing Waves,	Strathyre	Tel 01877 384361
Active Outdoor Pursuits.	Across Scotland	Tel 01290 420007
Highland Adventure Centre.	Knockshannoch, Glen Isla	Tel 01575 582238
Wilderness Adventure.	Based in Edinburgh	Tel 0131 4435898
Killin Outdoor Centre & Mountain Shop.	Killin	Tel 01567 820652

PERTHSHIRE / TROSSACHS / GRAMPIAN RIVERS
EASY/ TOURING RIVERS

RIVER TAY (Loch Tay to Aberfeldy - a great touring river with plenty of trip possibilities) (Aberfeldy to SCA Access Point) - (SCA Access Point to Grandtully) - the most famous rapids in Scotland!) - (Grandtully to Stanley) - (Stanley to Thistlebrig) RIVER TEITH - easy paddling and rapids near Callender

INTERMEDIATE/ ADVANCED WHITEWATER RIVERS

RIVER ALLAN - a spate run in central Scotland. RIVER BRAAN (Upper section to Rumbling bridge) - for when the lower Braan gorge is too high. RIVER DOCHART - a short trip above Loch Tay. GARBH GHAOIR - a remote trip at the head of the Tummel valley.
RIVER GAUR - a remote trip at the head of the Tummel valley. INVERVAR BURN - a steep tributary of the Lyon. KNAIKE WATER - an Allan tributary. RIVER LENY - more than just a one rapid wonder. RIVER LOCHAY - A nice grade 3 river.
RIVER LYON - a good medium grade trip with a harder section. WATER OF RUCHILL - a promising sounding trip. RIVER TUMMEL (Dunalastair Water to Loch Tummel) - an easier and more remote section of the Tummel. RIVER TUMMEL (Loch Tummel to Loch Faskally) - a year-round river near Pitlochry.

VERY DIFFICULT/ EXTREME WHITEWATER RIVERS

RIVER BRAAN (Rumbling Bridge to 'Braan Gorge') - a committing Tay tributary.

THE NORTHEAST / ABERDEENSHIRE RIVERS
EASY / MODERATE TOURING RIVERS

RIVER CALDER - easy with hard gorge.
RIVER DEE (Above Braemar to Potarch) - a beautiful river - (Potarch to Banchory) - (Banchory to Aberdeen).
RIVER DYE - adventurous tributary of the Feugh near Banchory.

INTERMEDIATE/ ADVANCED WHITEWATER RIVERS
ALLT A' GHARBH-CHOIRE   - a steep River Clunie tributary.
RIVER BLACKWATER   - a serious Grade 4 river draining the Cairngorms.
CALLATER BURN   - a spate stream feeding the River Clunie.
RIVER CLUNIE   - a short trip through Braemar.
RIVER FEUGH   - a short trip near the Dee.
RIVER NORTH ESK (Upper Section) - for when the North Esk is high.
RIVER NORTH ESK   - one of the best Grade 4 trips in Scotland.
RIVER TILT   - a rocky narrow river!

VERY DIFFICULT/ EXTREME WHITEWATER RIVERS
GARBH ALLT   - a Dee tributary.
RIVER LUI   - a short steep Dee tributary.
RIVER MUICK   - strenuous, tough paddle.
RIVER QUOICH   - steep and very narrow

Ski and Snowboard Scotland's 3 Valleys
Glenshee Ski Centre, Braemar, Aberdeenshire Tel 013397 41320

All the major transport operators offer cheaper deals for flights, car hire, train and coach travel. Skiing and snow boarding breaks in Scotland are now cheaper. An excellent range of packages offers an attractive winter break alternative. The snowfields at Glenshee stretch over 3 valleys and 4 Munros, with access to 40km of marked pistes, plus off piste skiing. With its diversity of pistes, Glenshee offers something for everyone. Beginners and novices are able to ski and snowboard on the nursery slopes next to the main car park, with an easy progression onto the seven lifts, which start at car park level. For intermediate skiers/snowboarders there are no less than 26 blue and red runs, varying from the long and exhilarating to the short and steep. Experienced skiers and boarders have two excellent black runs - the Glas Maol black or the mogul strewn Tiger, which has been a formidable part of the Scottish ski experience for years. In addition to the on-hill terrain, boarders also have access to a specially designed Fun Park at Meall Odhar. The Ski Centre offers superb on-site facilities, from garment hire through to mountain restaurants and cosy cafés. On the mountainside piste groomers keep the slopes in the best possible condition. Glenshee has an extensive on-site and up-to-date ski and snowboard hire, with a team of experienced technicians for both children and adults. Equipment can be booked in advance Glenshee Ski Centre Ski and Snowboard School has a team of BASI and BSF qualified instructors offering lessons for all standards of skiers and snowboarders.

Ski & Snow Board Schools & Hire
Cairnwell (2069 - 3502 feet)		Tel.: 01250 41320
Braemar Mountain Sports,	Braemar	Tel.: 01250 41242
Cairnwell Mountain Sports, Glenshee by Blairgowrie		Tel.: 01250 885238
Braemar Ski School	Glenshee	Tel.: 0468 517829

Perthshire, Southern Cairngorms & Lochnagar

1. Braincroft Lodge

Braincroft Lodge is a High Standard Conversion of a 19th century farmstead set in its own estate. The site includes a mountain bike course and private fishing. Recent additions include a conference/meeting and games room. The Lodge is located within a short distance of many local attractions.

Braincroft Lodge is located in central scotland on the A85, 5 miles west of Crieff and 1.5 miles East of Comrie.
Sleeps 56 in bunks – 10 family rooms, 1 twin double room. Bed only £10, Breakfast £1.50.

Braincroft Lodge, By Crieff,
Perthshire, Scotland PH7 4JZ
Contact: Barbara Jack
Tel: 01764 670140 Fax: 01764 679691
Email: braincroft@scottishlodge.co.uk
Web: www.scottishlodge.co.uk

BREATH TAKING VIEWS IN TRANQUIL, SPACIOUS FARM LOCATION.

2. Glassie Farm Bunkhouse

Brand new farm bunkhouse in fully renovated traditional building. Outstanding hillside location with tremendous views over Aberfeldy and the Tay valley. Outdoor activities available locally include White water rafting, Canoeing, Rock Climbing/Abseiling, Hill walking & Pony Trekking. Well equipped kitchen, dining room/lounge & drying room. Available for Groups and individuals. Open all day – all year
From Aberfeldy cross roads follow B846 over Wades Bridge, turn right for Strathtay by Ailean Chraggan Hotel, 800m up this road turn right to Glassie Farm

Glassie Farm, Aberfeldy,
Perthshire, PH15 2JN
Contact: Llinos or David Robertson
Tel: 01887 820265
llinosrob@aol.com
www.thebunkhouse.co.uk

OUTSTANDING HILLSIDE LOCATION, WITH FANTASTIC VIEWS.

3. Old Bank House Lodge

Centrally situated within two acres of ground. The Old Bank House is an excellent base for touring, provides a stopover location for travellers on the A9 and is close to many outdoor activities. This welcoming Lodge with its 16 seater lecture room is also available for group bookings.
Double beds in 4 rooms
Located just off the A9, the main road route north. 3 minutes walk from Pitlochry train station. The buses stop right outside our front gate.
Sleeps 48, 28 in bunkbeds, plus 5 twin/double rooms, and 3 family rooms. Bed only £10 to £12 – Breakfast available £1.50

82 Atholl Road, Pitlochry, PH16 5BL
Contact: Barbara Jack
Tel: 01796 470022 Fax: 01796 473628.
pitlochry@scottishlodge.co.uk
www.scottishlodge.co.uk

IMMACULATE, CENTRALLY LOCATED IN PICTURESQUE TOWN OF PITLOCHRY.

4. Gulabin Lodge

Where we are:-
Gulabin Lodge is on the A93 road at the Spittal of Glenshee - 20 miles from Blairgowrie and 14 miles to Braemar. Public transport: Trains and bus station:- at Pitlochry 22miles, Blairgowrie 20 miles and Braemar 14miles, Glasgow 100miles and Edinburgh 80 miles.
Sleeps up to 37 in hostel dorms & family rooms. £11 to £15b&b, family room £40. Group discount (10+) available. Booking advisable with 50% deposit

Cairnwell Mountain Sports, Glenshee, by Blairgowrie, Perthshire PH10 7QE
Contact: Gustav Tel: 0870 4430253
Free Phone 0800 783 0423
Mobile: 0778 941687.
Email: info@cairnwellmountainsports.co.uk
www.cairnwellmountainsports.co.uk

The Lodge is situated in the heart of Glenshee at the foot of Beinn Gulabin, offering the nearest accommodation to the Glenshee Ski slopes. We offer roller, nordic, telemark snowboarding, alpine skiing, and hire of equipment in house. Gulabin is also an ideal base for climbing, walking or mountain biking - whether you are a beginner or an expert.
Also on your visit you can try some of the other activities available, which include hang-gliding, paragliding, orienteering, abseiling, artificial ski slope skiing, team building courses etc.
There is a nine-hole golf course and Clay pigeon shooting nearby. Five minutes from the Lodge is the Spittal of Glenshee Hotel, which its friendly bar, can provide meals usually has entertainment in winter, on Saturday evenings.
The Lodge offers comfortable, budged priced accommodation for individuals, families and groups. There are free hot showers, rooms are equipped with wash hand basins, linen and the whole house is heated under floor.

5. Rucksacks Bunkhouse

We have a sauna, log fires, electric showers, central heating throughout, laundry facilities & good drying room. The surrounding area boasts 30 munros with a good network of tracks for mountain biking. Braemar is only 8 miles from Scotland's largest ski lift served area and local hills are excellent for ski-touring. Rucksacks is centrally located in village. Take road opposite the post office and bus stop. Proceed 30m beyond telephone boxes and take 1st right. OS43,GR149914. Sleeps 26 in one twin room, Dorms for 6 & 8, and Alpine Platforms for 10. £7.00 to £9.00.

15 Mar Road, Braemar, Aberdeenshire, AB35 5YL,
Contact: Kate Muirhead,
Tel/Fax: 013397 41517

EXCELLENT BASE FOR CAIRNGORMS, LOCHNAGAR, GLENSHEE.

Cairngorms, Spey Valley & Badenoch

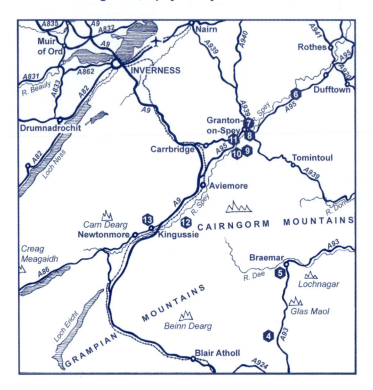

The high arctic mountain plateau and slopes of Cairngorm with the broad green valley areas of Badenoch and Strathspey are an all year round attraction to outdoor & wildlife enthusiasts, long distance walkers and world-wide independent travellers of all ages. The mountain village resort of Aviemore along with the newly refurbished ski facilities and furnicular railway on Cairngorm mountain act as a focus to activities in the Spey river valley. This stretches from the villages of Dalwinnie (near Drumochter Pass on the A9, north from Perth) and Laggan village (on the cross country route via Loch Laggan and the Monadhliath Mountains from Fort William) to the mouth of the River Spey where it reaches the Moray Firth.

The Drumochter Pass by **Dalwinnie** - (the meeting place of the cattle drovers in days gone by) is surrounded by steep mountains and crags, where the road can often be closed by snow for short times in winter. Dalwhinnie is now home to the highest distillery in Scotland with an excellent visitor centre open all year round offering you a "wee dram" as a taster to the classic malts which feature in the **Malt Whisky Trail** on Speyside.

Kingussie & Kincraig. Three miles north of Dalwinnie is Kingussie - the ancient Capital of Badenoch. Laggan village lies at one end of General Wade's most ambitious military road over the **Corrieyairack Pass** to Fort Augustus. The Highland Folk Museum is also in the village. Nearby, the ruins of **Ruthven Barracks** - built in 1719 - provide an evocative and timeless link to the Jacobite rebellion led by Prince Charles Edward Stuart - (better remembered as Bonnie Prince Charlie) in 1745.

Loch Insh offers a variety of outdoor and water pursuits. Nearby, the Cairngorm Gliding Club operates at Feshie Bridge Airstrip. Leault Farm which offers Sheepdog Demonstrations from the local shepherd and his dogs. The Highland Wildlife Park features wildlife which were all once native to the Highlands including the now extinct wolves, otters, lynx alongside some of today's more elusive inhabitants.

Standing beside the River Spey, in the foothills of the Cairngorm and Monadhliath Mountains, is a true land for all seasons. There are mountains, crags and glens, forests, moorland, rivers and lochs with facilities for both outdoor and indoor leisure activities. Winter sports for mountaineers and skiers, water sports, golf, fishing, rambling, climbing, mountain biking, tennis, bowls - all are within easy reach. In a land of timeless history and active adventure, visit ancient Highland Castles, malt whisky distilleries and forgotten drove roads.

Aviemore. From paddling a canoe or sailing on Loch Morlich in summer, to skiing down snow-covered ski slopes or climbing in the Northern Corries in winter, the area of Aviemore & Cairngorm offers unrivalled outdoor attractions whatever time of year you choose to visit. A visit to Rothiemurchus Estate ('The great plain of the pines') which has been owned by the Grants of Rothiemurchus for over 400 years is a must for families and those interested in Highland wildlife. Today over 50% of the Estate lies within the Cairngorm National Nature Reserve. The Estate includes a working fish farm, craft shop, farm shop, guided walks, wildlife safaris and clay pigeon shooting. Within the estate is Loch an Eilein with its ruined castle and visitor centre. The native forests of the Estate have always been harvested for their timber and the forests are a remaining fragment of the ancient native Caledonian woodland. The majority of the Estate is now managed for nature conservation. At Loch an Eilein Pottery there is the chance to throw your own pots or visit Inshriach Plant Nursery where you will find many rare heathers and Alpine plants for sale. At Coylumbridge there is 10-pin Bowling.

Further east is the tranquillity and scenic beauty of Glenmore Forest Park. The national outdoor training centre of Glenmore Lodge is located here with its multifacetted outdoor activity provision. The Forest park also features Loch Morlich Watersports Centre and the Glenmore Visitor Centre with its superb audio-visual presentation, forest gift shop and guided walks. The Cairngorm Visitor Centre houses the UK's only herd of free-ranging reindeer. Only nine miles from Aviemore is the Cairngorm Ski Centre with its year-round Mountain Railway carrying tourists, walkers and skiers high up the mountain to enjoy panoramic views of river and strath, corrie and moor. The Strathspey Steam Railway operates nostalgic trips between Aviemore - a Victorian building (typical of its era) and Boat of Garten from March to October and New Year.

Boat of Garten is known as the 'Osprey Village' and lies adjacent to the River Spey where a series of way-marked local walks can be explored. The Speyside Way Long Distance Route passes through the centre of the village, as does the Sustrans Scottish National Cycle Route 7. Excellent birdwatching opportunities in the surrounding woods and nearby Abernethy Forest are added attractions to the village.

Carrbridge & Strathspey. North-east of Aviemore towards Carrbridge, the River Spey twists and tumbles down through Grantown-on-Spey towards Aberlour and Craigellachie. Dating from 1717, the picturesque Bridge of Carr has long provided many visitors with a memorable image of Carrbridge. The village boasts woodland walks but it is best known today as the Highland home of one of Scotland's top family attractions – the Landmark Heritage Visitor Centre. Set in 12 hectares of pinewood, the centre boasts water slides and adventure playgrounds, not to mention a collection of nature trails, multi-media shows and a stunning tree-top walk.

At Nethybridge the ruins of the 700 year old Castle Roy can be seen as one of the first stone built castles in Scotland. A network of woodland footpaths and riverside trails provide a great opportunity to discover the natural beauty and cultural history of the area. Nethy Bridge is a quiet village next to ancient Caledonian pine forest. The backdrop of the often snowcapped Cairngorm mountains and hundreds of acres of Abernethy Forest (RSPB owned), Nethy Bridge spans the lower reaches of the River Nethy a mile before it reaches the River Spey, one of Scotland's foremost salmon rivers. The classic Telford designed bridge is in the heart of the village. A regular bus service operates between Nethy Bridge and Aviemore (11 miles) and Grantown on Spey (5 miles). The forest provides hundreds of square miles of walking and cycling on deserted tracks and a few single track roads. Canoeing and sailing centres are nearby, with numerous forest walks, swimming, go karting, horse riding, museums, and distilleries, most of which are open to the public. Nethy Bridge is situated half way between the Cairngorm and Lecht Ski Areas.

Dulnain Bridge is situated in the heart of Strathspey, centred around the 18th Century bridge. The surrounding forests of mature Caledonian pines contain many rare and interesting species. The bird list is headed by the endangered Capercaillie which are regularly seen. There are Scottish Crossbills, the beautiful Crested Tit, Buzzards, Eagles, and of course Ospreys. The Red Squirrel is native to these parts. Curr Wood on the south and east of the village has the country's largest population of rare linnea borealis or Twinflower. They share the forest floor with a tiny orchid called Creeping Ladies Tresses. The north end of Dulnain Bridge has a good display of a type of glaciated rock called 'Roches Moutonnees'. There are Pictish carved stones and two Stone Age coffins were found in the 1880's in a burial cairn in Curr Wood.

Grantown-on-Spey, the capital of Strathspey, was founded in 1765 by Sir James Grant. This fine example of an 18th century planned town has plenty to offer for all seasons. In winter when it becomes a winter wonderland providing ski-ing at the Lecht and Cairngorm – both 22 miles away. Winter climbing and walking is accessible in the Cairngorms mountains and plateau. In Spring the first green shows in the miles of walks in pine, birch and larch woodlands, wildlife wakens and salmon stir in the River Spey. The woods and forests are teeming with wildlife such as roe deer, capercaillie and crossbills. The RSPB Reserves at Abernethy and Loch Garten are only 10 miles away.

Grantown is close to the Revack Estate which combines attractive gardens, orchid house, nature trails, adventure playgound, a great day out for all the family. A visit should also be included to the historical ruins of Lochindorb Castle the ancestral home of 'The Wolf of Badenoch' born in 1343, the fourth son of Robert II and a grandson of Robert I 'The Bruce', Alexander Stewart was granted land in the area in 1371. From his island stronghold, Lochindorb Castle, he set out to raze the towns of Forres and Elgin in 1390 in reprisal for a censure by the Bishop of Moray. Following these events, Stewart was excommunicated and rapidly became known as the 'Wolf of Badenoch'. The Castle was dismantled by Royal decree in 1458 and its great iron door removed to Cawdor Castle where it can still be seen today.

Walking & Climbing in the
Spey Valley, Cairngorm Mountains and Morayshire Areas

This area includes the major mountain range of the Cairngorms, Monadliaths to the north west and the Drumochter hills to the southwest, However, in between these high mountains and moorlands there is extensive low level walking, on way marked forest tracks, in Forest Parks such as Glenmore by Loch Morlich which has become a mecca for walking – but there is much, much more on offer. There are three of Scotland's most well known hill passes which lead to the high mountain arctic plateau of the Cairngorms.

Easy Local Walks & Forest Walks

All the main villages in the area have an excellent net work of local walks, which vary in distance / time, for all levels of fitness, ability and aspiration and interest. Most of these walks are graded from easy to hard. There are excellent family walks for all ages near the villages of Dalwinnie, Newtonmore, Kincraig, Kingussie, Aviemore, Nethy Bridge, Boat of Garten, Grantown on Spey, Craigellachie through to Dufftown, Glenmore Forest, Rothiemurchus Forest, Insh Marshes and The Abernethy Forest

Long Distance Walks

The Speyside Way – 70 miles – allow 4-5 days. Start on the east bank of the River Spey in Spey Bay in the north – follow the River Spey south. There is no real need to commit to walking the whole length of the walk – short sections are excellent for one day walks in one locality. The walk finishes at Tomintoul.

Mountain Passes

The Cairngorms have several major hill passes which dissect the high arctic plateau – these were used by cattle drovers (and whisky smugglers) to reach markets and cattle trysts in the south at Stirling, Creiff, Dundee and Forfar beyond the "Highland Mounth". The Lairigh Grhu -The Corrieyarairack Pass - Ryvoan Pass - Glen Feshie – Glen Geldie – Braemar.

Mountain Days

The Cairngorm Mountain area is really a heavily dissected raised plateau which stretches for over 50 miles with more than fifty summits over 3000ft and four over 4000ft – Ben Macdui – Braeriach – Cairn Toul – Cairngorm – known collectively as the "Four Thousanders" and which can be completed in one day by the really fit!! The Monadliath Mountains. Lower than the Cairngorms – with expanses of heathery, featureless plateau with the noteable exception of Creah Meagheadh and Coire Ardair with its 500 m high crags alongside Loch Laggan – a winter climbing mecca.

Events

Walking Festival – Spirit of Speyside 17th – 20th October 2003 Tel 01343 820339
Corrieyairack Challenge – 5th July 2003 - Hill Walk – 17 miles.
Tel Badaguish Centre,   Aviemore   Tel 01479 861285
Climb Caledonia,   Inverness.   Tel 01463 667501
Scottish Orienteering Championships – August 2003

Rock & Winter Climbing. The Cairngorm area is home to major Scottish climbs – mostly with a fairly long walk in. The main rock and winter snow /ice crags are in the northern Corries of Coire an Lochain / Coire an Sneachda, Beinn Bhuird, Coire & Loch Etchegan, Loch Avon, Stag Rocks, Hell's Lum and the Shelter Stone, Braeriach / Cairntoul / Devils Point Amphitheatre, Loch Einich. **Crag Climbing**. There are a number of lower level, more accessible crags in this area. Creag Dubh near Dalwinnhe is a steep, moist crag on the road to Loch Laggan; Craigellachie crags above Aviemore; Chalamain Gap crags on the cross country route to the Lairig Ghru. **Climbing Walls**. Glenmore Lodge, By Loch Morlich. Climb Caledonia, Inverness Sports Centre, Tel 01463 667501

Guided Walks
Forest Ranger, Glenmore Forest Park Tel 01479 861220
Guiding & courses for walking, mountaineering , rock climbing and winter skills.
Mountain Innovations, Boat of Garten Tel 01479 831331
Ardenbeg Outdoor Centre, Grantown on Spey Tel 01479 872824 www.ardenbeg.co.uk
Woolly Mammoth Activities, Grantown on Spey Tel 01479 873716
Abernethy Trust, Nethy Bridge Tel 01479 821279
Lagganlia Outdoor Centre, Kincraig Tel 01540 651240
Glenmore Lodge, Loch Morlich, 01479 861256
Craigower Lodge, Newtonmore Tel 01540 673319
Hire of mountain equipment – boots, ice axes, crampons etc
Ellis Brighams, Aviemore Tel 01479 810175
Clive Rowland Aviemore & Inverness 01463 238746

Cycling & Mountain Biking in the Spey Valley and Moray Areas.

Extensive designated cycling trails are to be found in this area with the backdrop of the Cairngorm Mountains and Spey Valley. These run through the Speyside forests, in some of Moray's best scenery along the Moray coastline towards the north of Scotland. The trails and long distance routes widely vary in their length and difficulty – but there is something here for families, clubs, as well as dedicated "mountain bikers" of all standards.
Information
Trail Maps / information:- Available from The Recreation Ranger, Glenmore Visitor Centre, Forest Park, Glenmore. Tel 01479 861220
Forest Trails. These are to be found in the Glenmore, Rothiemurchus and Inshriach Forests.
Classic Mountain Bike Routes. From Aviemore there are a number of classic mountain bike routes – Ryvoan Pass, Glen Feshie, Corrieyairack Pass, The Burma Road which will give unique challenges to those more experienced cyclists. Long Distance Routes. Cycling is permitted on the Speyside Way – on quiet roads, footpaths and part of the old disused railway track. Or try the route along the Moray Coast taking in the Whisky Trail (about 180 km over 5-6 days from Inverness to Aviemore) The Cairngorm Circuit through the centre of the Cairngorms and Spey valley area.
Events
Corrieyairack Pass Challenge – 5th July 2003 Bikealthon – Kingusssie-Laggan Bridge
43 miles Mountain Bike Event e-mail paul.c@badaguish.org
Cycle & Mountain Bike Hire
Bothy Bikes, Aviemore. 01479 810111
Glenmore Mountain Bike Hire, Glenmore, By Aviemore. Tel 01479 861253
Speyside Sports, Aviemore. Tel 01479 810656
Cairngorm Mountain Sports, Aviemore. Tel 01479 861262
Rothiemurchus Estate, By Aviemore. Tel 01479 812343
Inverdruie Mountain Bikes, Rothiemurchus Visitor Centre, Tel 01479 810787
Cycle & Mountain Bike Tours / Days out – Guided and Self Guided.
Bothy Bikes, Aviemore Tel 01479 810111.

Canoe Sport in The Spey Valley Area

This area has a variety of paddling – on inland lochs, white water rivers and surfing beaches. The main rivers drain northwards to the Moray Firth from the Cairngorm mountains in the south. Here rivers tend to have a larger catchment area and are less steep than those on the west coast. The area is one of the few locations which has fine sandy surfing beaches which can be a good alternative to white water kayaking if the water levels are really low.
Sea Kayaking. There are local sea trips to explore the sandy shoreline of the Moray Firth Coast from Inverness eastwards – as well as the North side of the Firth into the Beauly, Cromarty, Dornoch Firths – and at the mouths of the Spey and Findhorn. **River Kayaking**. Sufficient water levels are mostly available in the autumn/ winter or when there is rain at other times - with paddling mainly concentrated on the rivers Spey and Findhorn. Many other short, steep rivers offer good spate river paddling. **Inland Lochs**. A few fresh water lochs to offer the opportunity to make really extended trips on open inland water on Loch Insh and Morlich.
Surf Kayaking. The Moray coast has some of the finest surfing beaches in the country with the main beaches at Sands End (Cullen); Spey Bay (by Fochabers); Lossiemouth; Scottish Surf Kayak Championships have been routinely held at Cullen in September.

Kayak & Canoe Instruction / river guiding/ hire – please check with the operator.

Ardenbeg Outdoor Centre, Grantown on Spey. Tel 01479 872824
Loch Insh Watersports, Kincraig Tel 01540 651272   Hire
Loch Park Adventure Centre, Keith Tel 01542 810334
Abernethy Trust, Nethy Bridge Tel 01479 821279
Lagganlia Outdoor Centre, Feshie Bridge, Tel 01540 651265
Loch Morlich Watersports, By Aviemore 01479 861221   Hire
Glenmore Lodge, National Mountain Centre, By Loch Morlich, Tel 01479 861256
Craigower Lodge, Newtonmore Tel 01540 673319
Adventure Scotland, By Aviemore. Tel 08702 402676
Woolly Mammoth. Tel 01479 873716
Highland Canoes, Aviemore. Tel 01479 810116   Canoe Outfitting / Hire

6. Ballindalloch Hostel

Unmanned hostel at the junction of the River Spey and Avon, Ballindalloch is an excellent base for white water canoeing, walking & cycling – and only 14 miles from the Lecth Ski Area for winter skiing. The Speyside way passes the door, and access to the river is just 100m

12 miles north of Grantown on Spey off the A95. Turn at the sign for Cragganmore and Speyside Way. Hostel is opposite telephone kiosk.

Sleeps 16 in bunkbeds. £8 per person per night.

Speyside Way, Ballindalloch, By Cragganmore AB37 9AB
Contact: Seretaray
Tel: 01540 651272 Fax: 01540 651208
office@www.lochinsh.com
www.lochinsh.com

IDEAL ACCOMMODATION FOR OUTDOOR ENTHUSIASTS SUMMER & WINTER

7. Ardenbeg Bunkhouse & Outdoor Centre (V)

The bunkhouse is ideal for individuals, families or groups who wish to base themselves amongst breathtaking scenery and superb facilities of the Cairngorms. Ardenbeg offers four warm and comfortable rooms, each with their own shower room, with two shared kitchens/diners for socialising. Outdoor pursuits instruction and equipment hire is optional. From Grantown traffic lights turn into Chapel Road, next to Chemist. At junction turn right into Grant Road. Ardenbeg is first house on left. OS 36, NJ 031278.

Sleeps 24 in rooms of 4, 6 or 8. family rooms available. £9.00.

Grant Road, Grantown-on-Spey, Moyayshire, PH26 3LD.
Contact: Rebecca Bird
Tel:01479 872824 Fax:01479 873132.
E-mail: enquiries@ardenbeg.co.uk
Web: www.ardenbeg.co.uk

SUPERB FOR INDIVIDUALS, FAMILIES OR GROUPS – OPTIONAL INSTRUCTION

8. Speyside Backpackers

Excellent hostel with full central heating and open fire in lounge. TV, Video & CD Player. Drying room with heater & dehumidifier. Kitchen with 2 hobs &large gas cooker. Rayburn & dishwasher & freezers/fridges. Separate dining room. Free off-road parking. Twin & Double rooms. Free tea & coffee. Close to shops (usually open 'til 10pm). Laundry Hostel on the square opposite Grant Arms Hotel. Regular buses from nearest railway station in Aviemore. By car – follow signs for Grantown-on-Spey from A9.
Sleeps 36 in bunks, and twin/family rooms. £9.50. Breakfast avail. £2.

15/16 The Square, Grantown on Spey, Morayshire PH26 3HG
Contact: Margaret Dingwall
Tel/Fax: 01479 873514.
r.lindsay@btinternet.com
www.scotpackers-hostels.co.uk

EXCELLENT. CLEAN HOSTEL LOCATED IN THE CAPITAL OF STRATHSPEY.

9. Nethy House

Excellent value accommodation on the Speyside Way. This large, centrally heated house, with bunk bedrooms sleeping 6 or less, allows complete flexibility for clubs, friends or groups of families. We've a residents' bar, games room, drying room; TVs, and lecture facilities. Local activities range from hill-walking and environmental studies. Catered / self-catered 6-85.

Past Post Office, over bridge, 1st large building on left. OS 36, GR 003997.
Sleeps 65, 61 in bunkbeds and 4 in single beds. £7.00 to £9.50. Breakfast available £1.50.

Nethy Bridge, Inverness-shire, PH25 3DS.
Contact: Richard or Patricia Eccles,
Tel/Fax: 01479 821370
info@nethy.org
www.nethy.org

OUTSTANDING HILLSIDE LOCATION, WITH FANTASTIC VIEWS..

10. Nethy Station

Sharing the Speyside Way car park we offer all a group could expect from a bunkhouse. It is well equipped & fully centrally heated. 2 bunkrooms sleep 9, 1 sleeps 2, plus an extra bedroom and storeroom with outside access. No groups sharing. Programme planning offered, all local activities. Catered/self-catered 6-22.
Past P.O., over bridge, turn left, turn 2nd right into lane & steps are on the right.
OS 36, GR 002997.
Sleeps 22 in bunkbeds. £7.50. Breakfast available £1.50.

Nethy Bridge, Inverness-shire, PH25 3DS.
Contact: Richard or Patricia Eccles,
Tel/Fax: 01479 821370
info@nethy.org   www.nethy.org

EXCLUSIVE USE ONLY. FOCUSED ON FUN AND FRIENDLINESS.

11. Dulnain Bridge Outdoor Centre

The Centre offers quality affordable accommodation for groups, in the Scottish Highlands, close to the Cairngorm, Aviemore and Grantown-on-Spey. It is an ideal base for outdoor activities, summer and winter sports, expeditions and adventurous training.
 Suitable for clubs, schools, organisations, armed forces etc. Groups are given exclusive use of the Centre and its facilities. Full Catering or Self-Catering available.
Nearby bar at local hotel

Sleeps 12 to 68 persons in bunks and single or twin rooms.

The Old Schoolhouse,
School Road, Dulnain Bridge,
Grantown-On-Spey, PH26 3NX.
Contact: Gill or Tony Sunde
Tel/Fax: 01479 851246.
www.scotlandoutdoors.com
info@scolandoutdoors.com

GROUP BOOKINGS ONLY.

12. Glen Feshie Hostel

Set in beautiful Glenfeshie with immediate access to the Cairngorms, this hostel is ideally placed for walking, climbing & cycling. In winter a perfect base for cross-country ski-touring. Watersports & pony-trekking are nearby for those with transport. Hot showers and good drying facilities, All bedding provided. Free porridge, other meals provided with notice. From Kingussie take B9152 to Kincraig, turn right down unclassified road, after 2km turn left on to B970 towards Feshiebridge. Cross River Feshie in 1.5km turn right at hostel sign, & follow for 4km. OS 35/36, GR 849009.
Sleeps 14 in bunkbeds and 2 singles.
3 family rooms. £9.00. FREE Porridge.
Breakfast £1.50 to £3.50

Balachroick, Kincraig,
Inverness-shire, PH21 1NH.
Contact: Jean Hamilton,
Tel: 01540 651323
glenfeshiehostel@totalise.co.uk

WARM FRIENDLY ACCOMMODATION IN A BEAUTIFUL LOCATION.

13. The Tipsy Laird

Purpose built 33 bedded hostel in prime location. Incorporating 7 bedrooms. Ideal for families. Full self catering kitchen, laundry. Unlimited showers, drying room. All Linen provided. Large garden to rear, picnic benches, barbecue, patio area. Tipsy Laird Restaurant, real ale pub next door. Food available 11am to 10pm. Daily breakfast & dinners for groups negotiable.

Mid-way up Kingussie High Street, enquire at the Tipsy Laird.
Sleeps 33 in 13 bunkbeds and 7 singles. £8.00.

66 High Street, Kingussie,
Inverness-shire PH21 1HZ
Contact: Bill or Jeanette Petrie
Tel: 01540 661334
Fax: 01540 662063

EXCLUSIVE USE ONLY. FOCUSED ON FUN AND FRIENDLINESS.

Ben Nevis, Glen Coe & The Road to the Isles
WE HAVE PLENTY OF SPACE – DO YOU HAVE THE TIME?

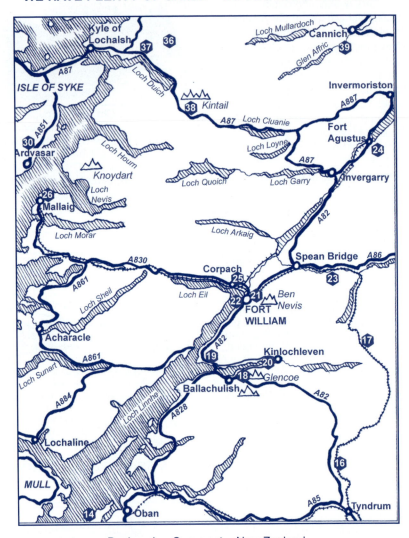

Backpacker Comment – New Zealand
"There is so much to explore and do in this area – so much like home - we only have a few
days in Scotland - but could stay a month in this one area.
"A real happening place all year round!"

Outdoor enthusiasts as well as world travelling independent backpackers all eventually find
their way to the well known and mostly long established hostels & bunkhouses in and around
the Highland West Coast town of Fort William. You will come for a wide variety of reasons. All
will get a warm, friendly welcome from the locally knowledgeable hostel owners. For the many
longstanding outdoor enthusiasts who repeatedly visit this premiere all year round mountain &
water activity area, the mountain icons of Ben Nevis, Glen Coe are attraction enough!
But we have much, much more to offer.

For only slightly lesser mortals, if it's sight seeing, touring, day tours or glimpses of a long history and culture you are after – we have plenty.

Trace on foot or mountain bike, the military roads, constructed by General Wade and others, to quell the "troublesome " warring Highland Clans. The steep sided rift valley of the Great Glen (Glen Mor) marks the route of St Columba as he made his way from the Island of Iona to Inverness to meet with the Pictish King Brude.

Touring and sightseeing by car is easy with quiet roads, easy parking in well placed view points and places of local interest ~ and relaxed driving at all times of the year.

Where we are?

Fort William, the main town and service centre in the area, is also a major transport and historical crossroads in the west Highlands.

Fort William itself is 102-miles/2 hrs north of Glasgow on the A82, via Loch Lomond side. Inverness is 77 miles north / 1 1/2 hrs, on the A82. Mallaig, 47miles/ 1-1/2 hrs to the west gives good access to Skye (ferry), the Small Isles & the Western Isles. Drive direct time from London is approx. 8hrs.

When to Come?

Ben Nevis, Glen Coe and the surrounding mountain & coastal areas have a weather system all of their own. Traditionally the very best weather is either mid May to late June or early September to early October when there is often unbeatable weather – maybe a little chilly in the early morning and late evening with alpine blue sky and brilliant sunshine by day – but not always.

What is there to see and do?

Either as an individual, couple, family or in a group there is plenty to do and see - without having to put your hand in your pocket – except for perhaps a bus or train fare or petrol.

There is also plenty to see and do if lack of inclination, energy or dodgy weather make you decide to give the Great Outdoors a miss.

The West Highland Museum – in the centre of Fort William. Clan Cameron Museum at Achnacarry (13 miles north of Fort William on the "back road" to Spean Bridge), Neptune's Staircase at Banavie on the Caledonian Canal (8 locks lift boats of all sizes over a distance of 500m by a height of 20m) are all well worth a visit. The Treasures of the Earth geological museum in Corpach village is certainly worth spending a few hours over. A visit to the Ben Nevis Distillery at Lochybridge, 2 miles N of Fort William gives a bit of "local flavour". In Glen Nevis, the visitor centre is a wealth of knowledge about local natural history history – as well as being a start point for the 6-8 hour Ben Nevis "tourist" Pony Track Route to the summit.

Despite its rich and ancient history the castles and remaining ancient monuments of the Fort William area tend to be a little thin on the ground. There are some magnificent remains of Clan castles, which tell tales of Clan history stretching from time immemorial to the present. Castle Toiram in Loch Moidart, Old Inverlochy Castle at Fort William, Kinlochmoidart House – near Castle Tioram – with its stunning display of rhodedendrums in May/June, Castle Stalker, near Appin, and Achnacarry Castle, lived in by the Camerons of Locheil – descendants of the loyal Jacobite supporters of Bonnie Prince Charlie Stewart in the 1745 uprising.

Out on the hills and moors lie the remains of the much older inhabitants – Picts, Irish Scots, Celts and Norse invaders who have all left their mark in some way – even if only in the place names left behind. Visit the vitrified forts at Onich and Glen Nevis, Standing Stones at Ballachulish, Onich and Kilchoan or the caves at Appin. The Parallel Roads of Glen Roy (15 miles to the NE of Fort William on the A86) are unique in the UK and world famous as glacial lake terraces left behind – 10, 000 years ago – when the glaciers melted after the last ice age.

Ben Nevis, Glencoe & Road to the Isles

Take a walk "on the wild side" by going seal watching, eagle spotting, get a glimpse of otters in rivers and sea lochs, watch for elusive ospreys fishing & soaring over their fishing grounds, If you are lucky see pine martins or wild cats in remote highland glens, or arctic fox, ptarmigan and snow buntings on the sub arctic mountain tops.

Take a cruise on Loch Linnhe to see Seal Island from the Crannog Restaurant on the Fort William waterfront. Loch Sheil Cruises, near Glenfinnan on the Road to the Isles & Mallaig takes you into the wilderness area to the west – or take an evening cruise with live music and a bar. The railway museum at Glenfinnan station is well worth a visit. The "Bonnie Prince Charlie" monument at the head of Loch Sheil marks the spot at Glenfinnan – more or less – where the Jacobite Standard was raised in 1745 at the start of the (failed) '45 Rebellion to claim the Scottish throne back for the House of Stewart. For excellent sandy beaches and unrivalled views out to the Eigg, Muck and the rest of the Small Isles, stop off in Arisaig. Here you will find a very different sea life/ information centre, which is well worth a visit. Mallaig has an excellent marine museum & sea life centre. This is the jumping off point for ferries to Skye, the Small Isles and the Outer Isles.

If the conditions are right, those who look for them may see the mythical monster of Lochaber. "Morag" – the supposed monster of Loch Morar, the deepest loch in Scotland. Or maybe the more famous but equally elusive "Nessie" in Loch Ness – who has reputedly left muddy foot prints on the A82 to Inverness!

At Invergarry on the A82 to Inverness there is a new visitor centre, which tells the story of the MacDonnells of Glengarry, as well as the now ruined Invergarry Castle.

Kinlochleven, to the east, at the head of Loch Leven, is a stopping off place on the West Highland Way. The village was established in 1904 with the coming of the aluminium smelter factory, which was fed by the hydroelectric Scheme in the village. With the recent closing of the Kinlochleven Smelter, the village is now being developed as an outdoor tourism centre.

On the road south – about 15 miles from Fort William is a bridge which has now replaced the old ferry at the village of Ballachulish. Take the ferry over to Ardgour, Ardnamurchan and Morvern at Corran narrows. The village of Glencoe is home to one of Scotland's oldest established mountaineering, rock climbing and ice climbing areas. As well as Scotland's longest established Ski Centre at White Corries – 12 miles south of Glencoe itself. There is now a Scottish Museum of Ski-ing and Mountaineering at the chairlift base station. In the village is an excellent Folk Museum. For an excellent night out try the famous climber's pub at the Clachaig Inn or the Four Seasons at Onich - both of which often have live music. The Grog & Gruel as well as Nevisport Bar in Fort William often have live entertainment.

A Highland Drover

Mountaineering, Winter Mountain Walking, Ice climbing, Rock climbing, Short walks, Long walks, High walks, Low walks - Summer and Winter

Springtime is an excellent time to be on the hills here – particularly for Rock-Climbing and Ridge Walking - from mid-April to mid-June, when the remains of the winter snows are still on the highest ridges and gullies. Days are longer and warmth returns to the crags. The classic ridge walks / scrambles on the longest mountain ridges are now alpine-like.

In the summer one hundred "tops" over 3,000ft (Munros) are within one hour's drive of Fort William. Some in really remote areas are many miles from the nearest road or public transport.

However, with some timetable planning, access is easily gained by taking the Glasgow train, which travels three times a day between Glasgow – Fort William – Mallaig (or to Oban from Crianlarich) and return, stopping at remote rail stations.

Waterfall Walks.

Often not far from off road parking facilities are several spectacular waterfalls in breath taking locations. Well worth a visit are: - The Steall waterfall and gorge at the head of Glen Nevis; the Witches Pool north of the well named "Dark Mile" at Achnacarry; Monessie Gorge on the river Spean, Roybridge; Laggan Dam is a spectacular sight in high water.

Lower Level and Forest Walks. For lower level, but spectacular views and wildlife follow part of (you do not have to walk all 70 odd miles to enjoy it) - the new long distance Great Glen Way from Corpach Sea Lock to Inverness. For the historically minded follow McBeth's burial route of 1056 from Inchree to Lundavra on the much later constructed Wades military road. **Mountain Glen Walks – Try these for size!** If you have enough previous experience, are well equipped and have done your homework – or get the services of a fully qualified local guide for a day or two. Walk the glens of the Three Lairigs out of Glencoe; Glen Loy through to Gleann Suilage; the head of Loch Arkaig through Glen Dessary to Loch Morar or Loch Nevis to Mallaig, are all very "wild" lower level walking.

Ben Nevis, Glencoe & Road to the Isles

See the glacial history at the geologically famous Parallel Roads of Glen Roy; the rugged and wild "Lost Valley" in Glen Coe – the hiding place of cattle thieves or Reevers; scramble or bike ride the "Devil's Staircase" from near the "Kings House", Glencoe- Kinlochleven; follow the Inverlochy Battle route of 1645 from Inverlochy.

The "Empty" Wilderness Areas. Experience the remote empty spaces in one of the most under populated areas in Europe with rugged scenery everywhere on Rannoch Moor, near Glenfinnan /Loch Sheil, Lochs Laggan, Arkaig and Knoydart areas.

Long Distance Walks. Fort William is the meeting of two national long-distant footpaths. The West Highland Way starts from Glasgow (100 miles) and the Great Glen Way heads north to Inverness (60 miles). Fort William is also the start of the unofficial "Cape Wrath Trail".

Rock, Ridge, Scramble – and Munros. Often covered in snow from November to April are the mountain range peaks of the Mamors above Glen Nevis; Creag Meagaigh by Loch Laggan; Bidean nan Bian – Stob Dubh – Buachaille Etive Mhor in Glencoe; the Grey Corries near Spean Bridge; the Monadh Liaths towards Newtonmore; rocky alpine like ridges of Ben Resipol and Garbh Bheinn of Ardnamurchan.

Rock-Climbing & Rock Ridges.

For experienced mountaineers – or with a qualified guide - try the classic mountain ridges / climbs of Aonach Eagach Ridge above Glencoe; and Crowberry Ridge, Curved Ridge on Buachaille Etive Mor; Carn Mor Dearg Arrete, or Tower Ridge, Ledge Route, Castle Ridge on the Ben – to name but a few. These are all of a more technical and serious nature.

Rock Crags. Rock climbing crags are found in Glen Nevis at Poldubh, on the north face of Ben Nevis and at many locations in Glencoe. Glen Etive has climbing on the Trilleachan Slabs. Garbh Bheinn – in Ardgour has airy, clean rock in a remote mountain location.

Winter Walking & Climbing. The area is a mecca for winter walking, winter mountaineering and ice climbing, mainly on the North Face of Ben Nevis, Aonach Mor and Glen Coe, between December and April. Those who have no previous experience of travelling in the Scottish hills especially in winter, are strongly advised to get at least a basic grounding in skills with locally based guides or instructors – before you venture out on your own. Check the weather and avalanche forecasts locally – do not take on more than your personal experience, equipment and winter daylight hours allow for. Leave word of where you have gone into the mountains – a route card is an excellent idea – leave a copy in your car with a registration number at your accommodation.

Ask for personal qualification of your guide/leader.

Dave Hannah,	Ballachulish.	Tel 01855 811620
Snowgoose Mountain Centre,	Corpach, By Fort William	Tel 01397 772467
Nevis Guides,	Roy Bridge.	Tel 01397 712356
Glencoe Outdoor Centre.	Glencoe	Tel 01855 811644
Climbwise,	Fort William,	Tel 01397 700765
Abacus Mountaineering,	Fort William	Tel 01397 701624
Glencoe Guides,	Glencoe.	Tel 01855 811402

Outdoor Retailers – Maps & Guide Books – Hire of Boots, Crampons

West Coast Outdoor Leisure,	Fort William.	Tel 01397 705777
Nevisport,	Fort William.	Tel 01397 704921
Ellis Brighams,	Fort William.	Tel 01397 706220
Glencoe Guides,	Glencoe.	Tel 01855 811402

Local book shops, Tourist offices well as local village stores stock some of the popular OS maps of the area. Ben Nevis & Glen Coe OS 38 & Landranger 41.

Paddlesports in the Glencoe, Fort William & Oban Areas

This area is a canoeing mecca – with over half of the best Scottish white water rivers within at most a 1 and 1/2 hour drive away. Importantly the area is not just a "white water" area. The rivers tend to be of a more technical nature (we are on the short, steep but higher side of the country) but there is plenty of scope for journeying by kayak or open canoe on the numerous inland lochs or miles of indented coastline. Access to the sea lochs is virtually at everyone's door step with the open sea some 30 miles to the south and west down Loch Linnhe; or to the north and west from the "Road to the Isles" at Arisaig or Mallaig – out to Skye and the Small Isles.

River Paddling

Fort William Area. As the centre of West Coast paddling the rainfall is recorded here on an average of 250 days per year. The rivers are mostly spate rivers which can be very quick to rise and fall – there is always the option to move to Glencoe or the Spean catchment area. The least technical option – but almost always with some water is the R. Lochy, with its spate tributary R. Nevis. The short steep R. Arkaig, R. Loy and Gloy are good choices when it has rained. **The Spean Catchment** offers paddling at almost all water levels as far as the dam release at Laggan Dam. The shorter tributaries of the Spean also provide great runs. The Roy is the most popular, but the Treig and Cour, are worth looking at. Further away - but not exessively so - to the north and west – the R. Oich is delightful moderate river about a 45 min drive from Fort William. The unpredictable dam released R. Garry – which flows into Loch Oich is a popular local paddling venue – despite its on going local access concerns. The R. Pattack (on the Loch Laggan road) and the R. Feochlan (on the 'back road' out of Fort Augustus to Inverness, near Whitebridge) are both established "experts" rivers – in the right water conditions. Also to the north the rivers of the **Spey Valley** – Spey, Findhorn etc are all easily paddled in a day from Fort William.

Glen Coe & Glen Etive. R. Leven (at Kinlochleven), R. Coe and Glen Etive river triple falls offer some of the best known water for "head bangers" to be found in Scotland. You need to be a competent white water paddler. In low water the tidal race at the Falls of Lora near Oban are an exciting alternative to fresh water paddling – but check the tides out first. To the south the R. Orchy and R. Awe (dam released) are larger rivers offering serious paddling at almost all water levels.

Instruction/ River Guiding - not residential. Canoe Hire & Outfitting.
Outdoor Retailers offering Canoe goods

Snowgoose Mountain Centre, Corpach,	Fort William.	Tel 01397 772467
Monster Activites,	South Laggan,	Tel 01809 501340
Glencoe Outdoor Centre,	Glencoe	Tel 01855 811350
Lochaber Water Sports,	Ballachullish.	Tel 01855 821 391
Linnhe Watersports,	Appin.	Tel 07721 503981

Sea Kayaking The West Highland coastline offers some of the best opportunities in Britain for journeying by canoe or kayak. Spectacular scenery, wildlife, unspoilt, really away from it all choice of destinations make this area a world class destination. The Spring month of May through to early September usually give the best and most settled weather. Strong tides are found in only a few places – mostly in and around the islands off Oban and round the **Ardnamurchan peninsula**. Arisaig has small islands and skerries close inshore.

The Isle of Skye with the Small Isles of Eigg, Rum, Muck and Canna lie further out. The sea Lochs of Loch Nevis and Loch Hourn used to access "Scotland's last wilderness" - the Knoydart peninsula – as well as being great places to explore by paddling.

Hire of Sea Kayaks and Instruction

Ardmay House Outdoor Centre	Arrochar	Tel 01301 702998

Mountain Biking in Ben Nevis, Glencoe & Oban Areas

Here, there is some of the best and most varied mountain biking to be enjoyed in a mountain environment. There are the well known trails in **Leanachan** forest starting at the Nevis Range Gondola car park - which is really ideal for families. The waymarked long distance Great Glen Cycle Route goes all the way to Inverness. Plus the world class Downhill track at Nevis Range – site of the World Cup Championships again in early June 2003

Great Glen Cycle Route is 73 miles long (117 km) from Fort William to Inverness, largely following the route of the tow path alongside the Caledonian Canal alongside Neptunes Staircase, Loch Lochy, to Loch Ness and Inverness. The whole route does not have to be cycled in one go – Local sections of a total of 10 miles can be done as one day cycle tours – some suitable for families – other sections are more robust.

Events

A number of Mountain Bike events take place at Nevis Range including World Cup events. In 2003 the Mountain Bike World Cup Championships will held over 31st May –1st June , with heats being held on the 30th May. Telephone for information – Event organisers 0131 557 3012 or www.fortwilliamworldcup.co.uk

Downhill Track & Mountain Bike 4Cross Track – presently the only one in the UK – will open to the public from 17th May to 14th September 2003

Information leaflets & web sites

Excellent Leanachan Forest TrailQuest leaflets are available from Forest Enterprise. Torlundy, Fort William, Inverness-shire. Tel 01397 702184.

Great Glen Cycle Route information is available from Forestry Commission, Forest Enterprise, Fort Augustus Forest District, Strathoich, Fort Augustus, Inverness-shire PH32 4BT. Telephone 01320 366322

Bike Hire

Bike Hire at Off Beat Bikes,	High Street, Fort William.	Tel 01397 704008
Bike Hire at Nevis Range,	Torlundy,	Tel 01397 705825
Glencoe Bike Hire	Glencoe	Tel 01855 811252.
Caledonian Bike Hire,	Banavie	Tel 01397 772373
Inchree Centre,	Onich, By Fort William	Tel 01855 821 287

Ski-ing at Nevis Range & Glencoe

Ben Nevis & Glencoe have two ski areas, the long established White Corries at Glencoe at the northern end of Rannoch Moor, and newer Nevis Range on the north facing slopes of Aonach Mor, beside Ben Nevis. Both centres are famous for maintaining good snow cover later into the season – often when other centres are closing. The slopes are generally open between Christmas and April, offering terrain suitable for all abilities.

Glencoe is an intimate centre, which boasts Scotland's steepest ski run, while Nevis Range offers the highest skiing in Scotland at 4006 ft and longest run of 2km

Nevis Range Ski & Snow Board Area, Fort William

Mountain gondolas carry skiers and boarders from the car park up to the slopes. The beginners' area is a stone's throw from the mountain restaurant, which offers a welcome refuge. There are 12 lifts and 35 downhill runs with a well-equipped ski & board hire on site offering a range of latest equipment. The Ski & Snowboard School is also on site offering a team of friendly, qualified instructors. The Nevis Range mountain gondolas run all year round (except mid November – Christmas), offering visitors an effortless ride onto Aonach Mor. Visitors can take a walk to one of the panoramic viewpoints, or relax in the mountain restaurant.

Visit www.nevis-range.co.uk for snow reports in winter, or telephone 01397 70582

Nevisport,	Fort William	Tel 01397 704921
Ellis Brighams,	Fort William	Tel 01397 706220
Nevis Range,	Torlundy	Tel 01397 705825
Ski & Snow Board School		
Nevis Range,	Torlundy	Tel 01397 705825

14. Ardentrive Farm Hostel

Warm comfortable cottage on working farm with a wide variety of animals – 10 minute boat journey from Oban – Splendid walks, spectacular views and a wide variety of wildlife. Self catering facilities in kitchen, but proprietor will cater on request, also washing machine & deep freeze. Large bath room & shower room, TV & oil fired Raeburn in lounge.

Please call for details of ferry timetable, directions & pick-up point.
Sleeps 10 in 4 bedrooms – no bunks. £8

Ardentrive Farm, Isle of Kerrera,
By Oban, Argyll, PA34 4SX
Contact: Joyce Tel: 01631 567180.
E-mail: joyce-glen@whsmithnet.co.uk

GREAT ISLAND HOSTEL

Ski-ing & Snow Boarding at Glen Coe
Located 74 miles north of Glasgow, Glencoe extends over 200 hectares and operates on the Meall A'Bhuiridh Massif, on the edge of Rannoch Moor above Glencoe village, some 20 miles from Fort William.
Ski-ing and snowboarding at Glencoe is a 3,636ft of mountain adventure with some of the best skiing in Scotland. From invitingly easy to surprisingly steep, from narrow gullies to wide open bowls. Glencoe has 2,600 vertical feet of superb natural terrain.
Glencoe Ski Cenre   Glencoe   Tel 01855851226
Web sites with Glencoe ski-ing
www.ski-glencoe.co.uk
www.ski.visitscotland.com

15. Ardmay House

BUNKHOUSE and CAFÉ in Loch Lomond and the Trossachs National Park
Located on the shore this 1850s fishing lodge provides premier accommodation at bunkhouse prices. £12 pppn includes bed linen, showers and drying room facilities.
The Café opens for breakfast and serves snacks and light meals throughout the day.

Also available
Open Canoes and Kayaks - Instruction and Hire
Guided Walks in the Arrochar Alps
Abseiling and Rock Climbing

For bookings and further information
contact   info@ardmay.co,uk
Tel 01301 702998
www.ardmay.co.uk

BUNKHOUSE IN LOCH LOMOND AND THE TROSSACHS NATIONAL PARK

16. West Highland Way Sleeper

Beautiful station building right on West Highland Way. Ideal base for Blackmount/Orchy munros. 2 unisex dorms sleeping 6 and 9. Great mattresses, all bunks with reading lights, privacy curtains. Modern en-suite facilities. Walkers licenced café open all day. Rail access to Corrour, Rannoch. Rafting, climbing, skiing all nearby.
By Car: Follow signs to Bridge of Orchy railway station on A82. By rail: Direct from Glasgow & Fort William. By Bus: Direct from Edinburgh, Glasgow, Fort William. OS50 GR300394
Sleeps 15 in bunks. £9
Breakfast from £3.75, Full board package £27.00

Bridge of Orchy Railway Station, Bridge of Orchy, Argyll, PA36 4AD
Contact Marion or Keith
Tel: 01838400548
info@westhighlandwaysleeper.co.uk
www.westhighlandwaysleeper.co.uk

COMFORTABLE CLEAN UNIQUE HOSTEL. MOUNTAINSIDE LOCATION.

17. Corrour Station Bunkhouse

The Bunkhouse was a Victorian railway station/ signal box, and still retains the character of its former use. It is situated at the core of a working/stalking estate, and is available throughout the year to groups or individuals. Restaurant available to the weary walker with cosy log fire (closed Wed) & shop for basic provisions. No smoking. Advanced booking advised.

Access is only on foot or via the West Highland railway line – step off the train and into the bunkhouse at Corrour Station.
Sleeps 14 in bunks. £10

Corrour Station, By Fort William, Inverness-shire, PH30 4AA.
Contact: Mrs E Vallance
Tel: 01397 732236 Fax 01397 732275
stationhouse@corrour.co.uk
www.corrour.co.uk

SPECTACULAR SCENERY WITH FIVE MUNROS ON THE ESTATE.

18. Glencoe Bunkhouses

Individuals or groups, climbers, walkers, canoeists etc. Basic accommodation. Some showers metered, some not. By mountains & river.
Self-cater or eat out at nearby pub. Walk historic area. Buses 1 1/2 miles away, train 15 miles – ideal for Backpackers. Hostel may change hands this year after 45 years of welcoming you all.

A82 Glencoe village, up main street, over hump back bridge, straight on 1.5 miles, large sign with squirrel & bunkbed on it.

Leacanturm Farm,
Glencoe, PH49 4HX
Contact: Hugh or Kathleen
Tel: 01855 811256
squirrels@amserve.net

OLD HOUSE, GREAT SCENERY, SELF-CATER.

19. Inchree Hostel (V)

Situated in Onich village, 4 miles north of Glencoe & 7 miles south of Ft William. Turn off A82 at Inchree and go up lane for 300 metres to hostel entrance.
OS41 GR02532
Glasgow to Ft William Citylink coach stop is 100m north of Hostel. Get off at Corran Ferry.

Sleeps 49 in bunks, family, twin, doubles and alpine. Rates from £7.50 (Bunkhouse group rate) & £9 to £13 (Hostel). Open 365 days. Breakfast from £2.75 to £5.95. Evening menu from 6pm – 9.30pm Bar open until late (Menu availability weekends only in winter)

Inchree Hostel, Inchree, Onich,
By Fort William, PH33 6SE
Contact: Paddy or David Heron
Tel/Fax: 01855 821287
E-mail: enquiry@hostel-scotland.com
Website: www.hostel-scotland.com

Located midway between Ben Nevis and Glencoe in 5 acres of private grounds. Perfectly located for touring and walking in the Western Highlands

* Self-catering hostel with group & family en-suite rooms. Doubles & twins also available in separate chalet unit.
* Bunkhouse hired to groups of 15 to 20 for their exclusive use – all facilities.
* Local area is renowned for superb hill walking, climbing, skiing & canoeing / kayaking.
* Enjoy picturesque forest, waterfall and beach walks from the door.
* Mountain bike hire and climbing wall on-site. Adventure activities run 500 metres away.
* Laundry & efficient drying rooms, barbeque area, internet access, weather forecasts.
* Walking, touring guides & maps provided for guests' use.

After your day out relax in our on-site bar and bistro whilst sampling Scottish Real Ales, Classic Whiskies and good food. Group & club functions fully catered for.

PEACEFUL LOCATION AMIDST A SPECTACULAR MOUNTAIN LANDSCAPE

Ben Nevis, Glencoe & Road to the Isles

20. Blackwater Hostel and Campsite

Situated in scenic village of Kinlochleven. Surrounded by Mamore mountains midway between Glencoe and Fort William. Ideal stopover for walkers, climbers, skiers and families. High quality bunkhouse accommodation. 10 rooms of 2,3,4 or 8 beds, all rooms en-suite & TV. Two fully equipped kitchens, lounge & Dining area. Drying room. Full Central heating. Private Parking.

In Kinlochleven, 7 miles from Glencoe, 20 miles from Fort William. OS41 GR189620 Sleeps 39 in bunk beds, some family rooms. Linen provided. £9 to £11.

Lab Road, Kinlochleven,
Argyll, PH50 4SG.
Caroline MacInnes 01855 831253
E-mail black.water@virgin.net
www.blackwaterhostel.co.uk

ALL ROOMS En-SUITE WITH TV'S - DRYING ROOM - RECENTLY REFURBISHED

21. Achintee Hostel

Beside the river in Glen Nevis this small hostel caters only for individuals, couples or families. Quiet rural location, offering a peaceful relaxing stay. Good drying rooms. Also B&B at farmhouse / self catering cottage (sleeps 2) by the week. Café/Bar with Internet access 100m

Bus/foot – across footbridge from Glen Nevis Visitor Centre. By Car – A82 (Inverness) – right into Claggan (traffic lights) – right before Spar shop, 2km to Achintee Farm – down drive.
OS 41, NN 125730.
Sleeps 14 - 3 Twin, 1 Triple & 1 Family room. £10 to £12pp.

Achintee Farm

Achintee Farm, Glen Nevis, Fort William,
Inverness-shire PH33 6TE.
Contact: Scot or Heather
Tel: 01397 702240
E-Mail: achintee.accom@glennevis.com
Web: www.glennevis.com

AT START OF BEN NEVIS FOOTPATH

22. Bank Street Lodge (V)

Situated 100m from the High Street. All bedding is provided with a fully equipped kitchen. Cutlery/crockery provided for self prepared meals – common room/lounge has tables/chairs and snack vending machine. Ideal location for climbing, walking (West Highland Way & Great Glen Way), and mountain biking.
Travelling from the south (A82) at second roundabout take 2nd exit then right hand filter lane. Take 1st left onto Dudley Road for 200m. From north – 1st left after Belford Hospital.
Sleeps 43, with twin, double & family rooms, £10 to £20 pppn. Breakfast £3.50 to £5.

Bank Street, Fort William,
Inverness-shire, PH33 6AY.
Contact: Kenny / John / Lynda
Tel: 01397 700070 Fax 01397 705569
www.accommodation-fortwilliam.com
info@accommodation-fortwilliam.com

IN THE CENTRE OF FORT WILLIAM

23. Àite Cruinnichidh (V)

2 miles east of Roy Bridge on A86 opposite the Glen Spean Lodge Hotel. OS 41, 301811. Sleeps 28 to 32 in bunk beds in 5 rooms of 4, 1 room of 6, 1 Twin and 1 Double/family room (en-suite). All bedding supplied. £ 9 per person/night

Contact: Gavin or Nicola
Tel: 01397 712315
Fax: 01397 712013
e-mail: info@highland-bunkhouses.co.uk
Web www.highland-bunkhouses.co.uk

1 Achluachrach, By Roy Bridge, Inverness-shire PH31 4AW.

Warm comfortable, friendly country hostel in converted barn. Set in stunning mountainous surroundings near Fort William. Ideal location for walking, climbing, canoeing, and mountain biking, with 7 rivers for paddling within 20 miles of Àite Cruinnichidh. Extensive cycle routes and the longest downhill mountain bike track in the UK nearby. We can advise you on walking and cycling routes. Maps are also available.
Additional facilities include en-suite family/double room, dark room, drying room, reading/quiet room, sauna, a 45 sq metre fully equipped meeting/seminar room for course work, slide shows or ceilidhs. There is also a garden for outdoor games or for practising outdoor skills.
Bike Hire Available
We can also offer a lock up for bicycles and gear, a pick up from the local train or bus, excellent parking and information on the local area. Outdoor activities can also be arranged from Àite Cruinnichidh and for groups food, fruit and veg can be ordered in advance of your arrival.
Unfortunately we cannot organise the weather!

WARM COMFORTABLE FRIENDLY - STUNNING SCENERY - SAUNA

24. Morag's Lodge

Highland hostel, situated in its own wooded grounds on an elevated position overlooking Loch Ness and the village of Fort Augustus. Large comfortable bunks in mostly en-suite rooms, breakfast and dinner available at reasonable cost, cosy bar with open fire on site, fully licenced.

From the village centre go North towards Inverness past the filling station, turn first left up Bunnoich Brae, the hostel is at the top of the hill on the left. GR 377 095

Sleeps 53 in bunks, plus 2 twn/dbl rooms. £12 to £14 per person.
Breakfast available £2.

Bunnoich Brae , Fort Augustus, Inverness-shire PH32 5DG
Contact: The Manager
Tel: 01320 366289
Fax: 01320 366702
morags@radicaltravel.com

LOCH NESS, COMFORTABLE BEDS, FRIENDLY SERVICE, EN-SUITE ROOMS.

25. Smiddy Bunkhouse (V)

Transport. Direct main line rail/coach links to Glasgow/Mallaig/London. Corpach rail station 2 minutes walk away. Pick up available from Ft. William.

Where we are. Located in village of Corpach - 4 miles north & west of Fort William. Take A82 north out of Fort William. Turn left on A830 to Mallaig. Look for the rail station and Snowgoose sign on the left in Corpach village.

Sleeps 26 in bunk beds in rooms of 4, 6 and 8. Fully self catered – no food provided. Prices From £7 to £10 ppp.nt. Group Rates & Family Rooms available. Electricity charged extra in winter.

Station Road, Corpach
Fort William, PH33 7JH
Inverness-shire
Contact: John & Tina Cuthbertson
Tel: 01397 772467   Fax: 01397 772411
Web www.highland-mountain-guides.co.uk
info@highland-mountainguides.co.uk

A friendly, family welcome at our comfortable, mountain based hostels sleeping 12 or 14. Loch-side location overlooking the extreme SW end of the Caledonian Canal. Ben Nevis 4 miles.
Providing full self-catered facilities with a pine clad interior to give a cosy, friendly atmosphere in a convenient village location. HOT showers. Fully equipped kitchens available at all times, (food available from local shop).
Use of 2 efficient drying / laundry rooms. Bedding provided inclusive in price. Fully heated for all year round use. Outdoor information / Daily Snow & Avalanche Reports. Maps for hire. Stunning mountains & water at the doorstep at the meeting of the Long Distance West Highland Way, Great Glen Way & Cycle Route.

* Excellent Group & Family Accommodation.
* Use of full meeting/lecture facilities by arrangement.
* The premier base for all mountain based adventure activities – winter mountaineering , ski-in, summer Rock climbing – hill walking – scrambling.

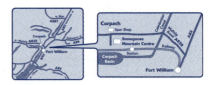

STUNNING BASE - WALK,CLIMB,CANOE,SKI,SAIL

26. Sheena's Backpakers Lodge

The Backpackers' Lodge in Mallaig offers a base from which you can explore the Inner Hebrides, the famous white sands of Morar and the remote peninsula of Knoydart. It also has a beautiful garden café where you can relax and watch the fishing boats.

100yds to right of railway station, 150yds from ferry terminal.
Sleeps up to 12 in bunks.   £11

Cafe on premesis

Harbour View, Mallaig,
Inverness-shire PH41 4PU.
Contact: Sheena Tel: 01687 462764 Fax
01687 462708

COMFORTABLE, FRIENDLY, COAL FIRE, ROMANTIC, HILLWALKING, BEACHES.

Scottish Hostels
Enhanced Entries
2003/4

The view down
Little Loch Broom
towards
Badrallach Bothy.
(Hostel 44 Page 57

Inchnadamph Lodge,
Loch Assynt & Quinag
(Hostel 46 - Page 62)

Bisgoes Hostel &
Cottages, Isle of
Westray, Orkney
(Hostel 52 - Page 69)

The Small Isles, Skye and the Western Isles

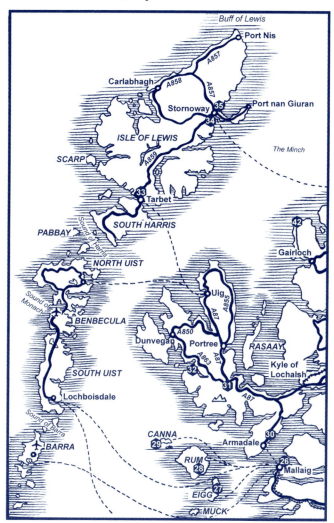

The Small Isles.

These Islands include Rum, Eigg, Muck & Canna – all are reached by ferry from Mallaig or Arisaig. Day trips operate from both ports allowing a few hours ashore – but why not stay awhile on one of these idyllic islands..

Rum. Owned & managed by Scottish Natural Heritage, Rum is a haven for plants & wildlife, and is popular for walking – the mountains on the island are over 2500ft – but always seek advice from the reserve manager. Hostel /B&B accommodation is available at the impressive Kinloch Castle (page 48), which also has a small Bistro.

Eigg. The second largest of the small isles, Eigg was recently bought into community ownership. The unusual shape of the island results from a flat-topped basalt peak, with 3 near vertical sides.

Canna. Owned and managed by the National Trust for Scotland, Canna is run as a single working farm, but is also a haven for birdlife – including Puffins. The walking on Canna is more gentle than on Rum, the highest point a mere 700ft, but offers great views out to Skye & back to Rum.

Muck. The smallest & flattest of the islands, Muck is ideal for those who enjoy getting away from it all. The craft shop and tea room have a wide range of meals available.

The Isle of Skye.

Thought by many to be the most scenic of the west coast islands, Skye is an ever popular destination. The Cullin mountain ranges includes some of the best peaks in the Highlands, and are a major draw for serious walkers and climbers all over. The island includes spectacular coastline, and many unusual rock formations. Some of the key attractions include the classic view of the Cullins from Elgol – a 14 mile drive down a twisting single track road. The green a fertile Sleat Peninsular provides a contrast to the rugged mountainous terrain of the rest of the island. The Clan Donald Visitor Centre is wort a visit at Armadale Castle. Broadford & Portree are the two largest settlements on the island, and now offer a wide range of services to the visitor.

The Isle of Raasay is reached by 15 minute car/passenger ferry from Sconser – with frequent sailings. The island offers superb walking, and exceptional views to the Torridon mountains on the mainland, and the Cullins on Skye itself. Bike hire and activities are available at the Raasay Outdoor Centre.

Portree was once a busy fishing port, but now the much quieter harbour is overlooked by a row of colourful houses, with a steep road leading up to the main village square. Just north of Portree the 'Old Man of Storr' – a pinnacle of rock detached from the cliffs behind – provides a popular walk, and a scenic photo stop.

The small port of Uig is the departure point for CalMac ferries to Isle of Harris. A few miles north the ruins of Duntalum castle are a dramatic sight set on the top of the sea cliffs. Dunvegan Castle, home to the chief of Clan Macleod, is open daily through the summer. Neist Point, where there is a very plesant walk along to the lighthouse at the most westerly point on Skye. At Carbost the Talisker Distillery is a popular stopping point as the tours include a free dram! The area around Portnalong is dominated by the views south back to the Cullins. The mountains are accessed from Glen Brittle in the west, Sligachan (on the Portree - Broadford road) or from Elgol in the south. Be prepared for these are some of the most exposed & rugged mountains in Scotland – care is essential.

Transport to / from Skye, and around the Island.

Despite the construction of the 'Syke Bridge' from Kyle of Lochalsh to near Kyleakin, there are still two ferry routes over the sea to Skye. From Mallaig there is a regular CalMac service to Armadale in the south west, and during the summer from Glenelg there is a small private ferry taking a maximum of 6 cars to Kylerhea (just south of Kyleakin). The Bridge is the most common crossing point, used by all the major bus firms, and ideal if you have arrived in Kyle of Lochash via the scenic West Highland train line from Inverness. If arriving from the Westen Isles there are CalMac ferries from Tarbert & Lochmaddy to Uig.
Public Transport on Skye is possible to most areas – using the postbus service to supplement the standard bus routes. The service is very limited at weekends.

Car Hire is available in Broardford (Sutherlands Garage Tel: 01471 822 225) & Portree (West End Garage Tel: 01478 612 334). For the energetic Bike hire is also available from Sutherlands Garage, from Island Cycles in Portree (Tel: 01478 613 121) and from Barbara at Orasay, Uig (north Skye ferry terminal) (Tel: 01470 542316 or 07968 652267).

The Western Isles

A chain of islands 130 mile long make up the Western Isles. The main islands are Lewis & Harris, North & South Uist Benbecular and Barra. Much of the interior is a wild land of bogs and rocky outcrops, but the coastline and beaches are some of the best, and Harris in particular has great mountains.

Lewis. Lewis has many spectacular sandy beaches, a rugged coastline and a low-lying landscape covered by a blanket of peat bog. The underlying rock, Lewisian gneiss, is thought to be 2900 million years old - half as old as the Earth itself. Most visitors come to see the Calanais (Callanish) standing stones (on the west coast), but it is also a good area for fishing, cycling, walking and bird watching. There are many other standing stones and archaeological monuments to visit too, and many of the small roads around the coastline are well worth exploring. The landscape and history of Lewis, together with the hospitality of its people provide a wonderful escape from the pressures of modern life. With luck you may even see plenty of wildlife – such as otters, seals, eagles or dolphins. In the summer months there are many colourful wild flowers to be seen on the machair. The heather is a picture of purple in late summer when in full bloom. The main town of Stornoway is a commercial centre for all the Western Isles, and has a full range of shops & other facilities.

Traditional Black House – Western Isles

Harris. Although geographically Harris is actually the lower third of the island that also includes Lewis. It is however consider a separate island, and has an diverse scenery comprised of mountains, extensive white sandy beaches to the west, and a rugged rocky landscape to the east. The main settlement is Tarbert, and it offers a range of tourist services – as well as being the port for ferries to Uig on Skye. North Harris includes the most mountainous areas of the Western Isles, and is the destination for hillwalkers.

North Uist. The most northerly of the southern islands in the chain, North Uist is low lying and covered in lochs & lochans. Its popular with fishermen and wildlife enthusiasts. Benbecula, South Uist & Barra complete the chain of major islands. South Uist boast a couple of reasonable hills (2000ft) and an extensive sandy beach along the entire length of the west coast. The small island of Barra offers a taste of everything the Western isles has to offer, beaches, acheaology, crofting townships, and peat covered hills. The airport is on the beach!

Skye, Small Isles & Western Isles

45

OUTDOOR HEBRIDES & SKYE
Isle of Lewis, Harris, North & South Uist, Benbecula, Barra, Skye and The Small Isles of Eigg, Rum, Canna

The Hebrides, Skye and the Small Isles are a natural area for adventure - a playground in an unspoilt wilderness "on the edge" with extensive activities for such a small area. For the seasoned outdoor adventurer and absolute beginner, there are experiences and activities to cater for all on the sea by kayak, sail board, dinghy or yacht; on land – with open moorland & hills, by cycle or on foot; on crags, sea stacks and cliffs; and even in the air!

Adventure challenge events highlight the world class outdoor opportunities on offer:-
The Hebridean Challenge (June 23 -28 2003) one of Europe's toughest adventure-races, is a week long race the length of the island chain in kayaks, bikes, and by swimming and running. Four half marathons and two challenging hill races take place every year; the International Hebridean Surf Festival with world champion surfers competing; the annual Sea and Surf Kayak Symposium in North Uist (August 21 -25 2003) is a gathering of sea kayaking enthusiasts of all levels.

Surfing
Positioned on the edge of the North Atlantic receiving swells from any direction and with a range of white shell sands, reefs, pebble shores and beach breaks, the Outer Hebrides have the most consistent surf in Europe. In certain swells on some beaches there will be tidal rips and strong currents – always get local information or contact the coastguard. Never surf alone especially on an unfamiliar beach and check the local weather system.

Surf Beaches on the north and west coasts. For surfing information contact Stornoway Canoe Club – web site on www.stornowaycanoes.co.uk – links to surf indicators/ weather etc.

Sea Kayaking. The maze of inlets, cliffs, hidden coves, wide sandy beaches, sea stacks and arches, caves, high soaring cliffs make the Hebrides and Skye part of a world class sea kayaking destination. Skye is a bit short on the sandy beach and surf scene it is a start point for the crossing of the Minch, along with paddles the Small Isles of Eigg, Canna, Muck and Rum.. For the ultimate expedition experience join a supported journey to the remote St Kilda island group.

Events
Lewis Surf Gathering – Isle of Lewis – Contact Andy Spinks Tel 01631 710317

Cycling in the Skye & The Western Isles
The chain of the six main islands offer a compact, very varied and unique cycling experience – from challenging off road cycling to gentle routes following sandy beaches fringed with machair grasses. The smaller off shore islands are linked by causeways. There is always the choice of taking a day trip by cycle then returning to base by bus.

One and two day cycle routes
Lewis, Uig to Stornoway Cycle Route – 33 miles or a 66 miles circular trip; N Uist - Berneray - S Harris – the islands are linked by ferry; Isle of Barra – a circular route fromCastlebay via Vatersay - short day - 20 miles; Calanish Route – about 30 miles round trip on quiet roads starts in Stornoway – via the ancient Calanish Standing Stones; Drinishade to Isle of Harris - 30 miles.

Hebridean Long Distance Cycle Route – 191 miles – 6-7 days – by train or cycle Inverness –Garve – Ullapool then by ferry to Stornoway – the route start – through the islands south to Lochboisdale and on to Isle of Barra.

Walking & Rock Climbing in the Western Isles & Skye
Rock Climbing. Here the world's oldest rock comes to the surface. There are acres of unclimbed rock – often in an empty landscape – with sea cliff climbing and sea stacks to mountain crags the most well know at the Sron Ulladale on N. Harris. The Isle of Skye is the highest, most mountainous area in the area with ancient Gabbro rock forming the long sharp ridges and classic rock faces of the Cuillins.

The Cuillins are probably the most impressive mountain ridges range in the UK – the climbing here is comparable to the Alps – except for the height. The Skye Ridge Traverse is a classic high level route over about 7km – but will take at least 2 days with a "bivy" on the ridge. Other classic routes are on the famous Cioch Buttress in Coire an Lagan along with Pinnacle Ridge on Sgurr nan Gillean. The Isle of Rum has some climbing on the Askival range. The Western Isles have numerous rock outcrops – far too may to list here – some only accessible by charter boat – especially on the sea stacks south of the islands off Barra.

Walking Routes

Skye & The Small Isles
Skye, Rum and Eigg – because of greater size – offer good local walking – try the walk to the Sgurr of Eigg. The Cuillins of Rum – with the Viking names of Orval, Trollval, Hellival and Askival are the remains of an ancient volcano.

Western Isles
The Hills of Uig and Park are of most interest in Lewis with height of 570m. Harris is the base for some of the best lower level walks in the area, centred on Tarbert. North Harris has 9 summits over 600m in height with Clisham the highest at 799m. There are many old stalkers' paths which avoid much of the boggy ground!

Travel to the Western Isles

By Air.
There are flights to Stornoway from Inverness (BA & Highland Airways (01852 701282)) & Glasgow (BA). There are also flights to Barra & Benbecular from Glasgow (BA).

By Ferry.
The main routes are from Ullapool to Stornoway, and from Uig on Skye to Tarbert and Lochmiddy (summer only) (all CalMac) There is a summer /occasional winter service from Oban & Mallaig to South Uist & Barra.

Travel between the Islands.
By Air. There are flights between Barra, Benbecular & Stornoway – operated by BA.
By Ferry. From Leverburgh (Harris) to Otternish (N Uist) – frequent sailings. There is a daily crossing from Barra to South Uist, and from South Uist to Isle of Eriskay.

By Bus. Buses operate on the main routes across the islands. There are no buses, ferries or flights on Sundays.

By Car/Cycle. The easiest way to explore the islands is with your own transport. Car hire is available in Stornoway (Tel 01851 710548 / 703760 / 706939/ 702984), Harris (Tel: 01859 502221 / 520460), Benbecular (01870 602191 / 602818) & on Barra (01871 810243 / 890366).
Cycle Hire in available in Stornoway 01851 704025, Lewis 01870 620283 & Barra 01851 810 284

27. The Glebe Barn

Enjoy our well equipped self catering accommodation. Superbly comfortable with fantastic views, spacious living area, maple floor, woodburning stove, all facilities. Situated 1 mile from pier, shop, restaurant (frequent music sessions). Appreciate wonderful walks, soaring eagles, 'singing sands', beautiful beaches, fascinating archaeology and geology. Available exclusive let.
Ferries - 1 hour from Mallaig (5 times a week 01687 462403) or from Arisaig, daily (not Thursday, Summer only 01687 450224).
Sleeps 24 in a mix of bunks and single beds. Bed from £9.50 to £11, whole hostel from £120. **Prior booking essential.**

The Glebe Barn, Field Study Centre & Independent Hostel, Isle of Eigg, Scotland PH42 4RL
Contact: Simon or Karen Helliwell
Tel/Fax: 01687 482417.
E-mail simoneigg@cs.com
www.glebebarn.co.uk

FANTASTIC FACILITIES, VIEWS, BEACHES, WALKING, BIRDWATCHING & CULTURE.

28. Kinloch Castle – Rum

Kinloch Castle was gifted to the nation as part of the Nature Reserve on the Isle of Rum. It is owned and operated by Scottish Natural Heritage. The castle was built as recently as 1897, in the highest standards of the time – it includes top quality timber work and panelling. Almost all of these features remain, and the Castle is open to accommodate visitors in both Hostel accommodation and more superior private rooms.

Guided tours of the reserve are available.

Kinloch Castle, Isle of Rum.
Reservations are essential
Tel: 01687 462037

GREAT ACCOMMODATION ON A SPECIAL ISLAND

29. Kate's Cottage – Isle of Canna

Kate's Cottage is a small converted cottage on the hill above Canna harbour. The cottage provides very basic accommodation in three rooms – common room/kitchen and two bedrooms. The toilet & shower is in an extension and accessed separately. This is a very peaceful location with stunning views to Rum and the Cullins.

OS 39, GR 266055. Acces only by ferry from Mallaig 4 days per week.
Sleeps 6 in just 3 bunkbeds.
£6 per person per night.

Kate's Cottage, Isle of Canna,
Inverrness-shire PH44 4RS
Contact: Winnie MacKinnon
Tel: 01687 462466

BEAUTIFULL LOCATION ON A BEAUTIFULL ISLAND

30. Flora MacDonald Hostel

Hostel – 2 rooms with bunk beds for 20. Pine lodge – 3 private rooms each containing accommodation for 4 persons. Pine bunks. Modern kitchen, TV, laundry, hot showers, central heating. Standing in own private grounds in 'Garden of Skye' overlooking Sound of Sleat towards Loch Nevis. Open all year. Parties and groups welcome

3 miles north of Armadale Ferry on A851. 20 miles south of Skye bridge. Free transport from Armadale pier to hostel. OS , GR NG 60/70. Sleeps 24 in bunks and one family room. Bed only £8 - £12.50 (private room),
Breakfast available on request £2.50.

The Glebe, Kilmore, Sleat,
Isle of Skye. IV44 8RG
Contact: Peter MacDonald
Tel: 01471 844440/272 Fax: 844440
E-mail: peter.macdonald@talk21.com
www.flora.plus.com

BUNKHOUSE IN LOCH LOMOND AND THE TROSSACHS NATIONAL PARK

31. Sligachan Bunkhouse

The Bunkhouse overlooks the 'Black Cullins' and is an ideal base for exploring the magnificent mountains of Skye. Several routes up the peaks pass the bunkhouse, and the path to 'Loch Coruisk' can be seen from the Verandah. The Bunkhouse is surrounded by peaceful mountain scenery on a track easily accessible by car. It is a 5 minute walk from the bus stop at Sligachan. Hotel & Bar nearby. Buses run to Sligachan from the mainland and Portree.

Sleeps 20 in 2 four bed and 2 six bed rooms. £9 to £12 – Group rate £120/night. Breakfast & other meals available at Sligachan Hotel.

Sligachan Self Catering, Sligachan, Isle of Skye, IV47 8SW
Contact: Catriona Coghill
Tel: 01478 650204 Fax 01478 650207
reservations@sligachan.co.uk
www.sligachan.co.uk

COMFORTABLE CLEAN UNIQUE HOSTEL. MOUNTAINSIDE LOCATION.

32. Skyewalker Independent Hostel (V)

OS 32, GR 348348. A863 from Sligachan 5 miles to. B8009. Travel 6 miles through Carbost to Portnalong. Turn left onto Fiscavaig Road and Hostel is 5oo metres on right. Several buses now serve Portnalong, all picking up at Sligachan. Free transport can be provided from Sligachan outwith the scheduled bus times. Ring hostel.
Sleeps 36 in 2, 4, 6, 8 & 10 bedded rooms.
Bed only from £8 to £9.50.
Breakfast from £1.50

Old School, Fiscavaig Road, Portnalong, Isle of Skye IV47 8SL.
Contact: Trevor / June Mann
Freephone 0800 0277059
Fax: 01478 640420

E-mail: skyewalker.hostel@virgin.net
Web: http://freespace.virgin.net/skyewalker.hostel/index.htm

Amongst Scotland's best hostels.
Whether your interests are climbing, walking, wildlife or just enjoying the beautiful views, the Skyewalker Independent Hostel offers comfortable, centrally heated accommodation with all amenities. The perfect base for outdoor activities with hill, moor and water all combining into spectacular scenery with a warm welcome, hot shower and comfortable bed to finish the day. For those interested in fishing there are beaches (with and without rocks) nearby and trout fishing is possible by arrangement
There is well-stocked shop and an excellent licensed café on site and the village Post Office is situated within the Hostel
For those who prefer it we also have a small campsite within the 4 acres of grounds which also provide a good playing area for children who are very welcome
The village pub is 5 minutes walk

STUNNING BASE - WALK,CLIMB,CANOE,SKI,SAIL

33. Rockview Hostel

Rockview Bunkhouse is a newly renovated two-storey building ideally situated in the main village of Tarbert. There is a well equipped kitchen, a lounge, showers & dorms.

The bunkhouse is in close proximity to all amenities. It is also ideal for those travelling via late or early ferries as it is only a two minute walk from the ferry terminal.

Sleeps 32 in mixed dorms, and a female dorm.

£9 per person per night

Rockview Bunkhouse, Main Street,
Tarbert, Isle of Harris,
Western Isles, HS3 3DJ.
Contact:
Mairi Fraser 01859 511240
Valerie Murray 01859 502272

34. Fairhaven Bunk House

Experience the islands of Lewis and Harris from a central location at affordable prices. Stay with us at "Fair Haven", a rambling town house with lots of facilities. Chill out in a friendly and informal ambience. Enjoy the remote reaches of these beautiful islands or simply relax and take pleasure from a carefree and memorable environment. Local knowledge, information, suggestions and directions freely available

Centrally located in Stornoway.
Bunk rooms, family, double, twin and single rooms available. £10 to £15 (single) per person per night. All meals available at extra cost.

28 Francis Street, Stornoway,
Isle of Lewis, Scotland, HS1 2ND
Contact: Tel 01851 705862 / 840337
Fax : 01851 870235
hebsurf@madasafish.com
www.hebrideansurf.co.uk

AN IDEAL BASE TO LEARN TO SURF.

35. Laxdale Bunkhouse

Located 1.5 miles from Stornoway within Laxdale Holiday Park the bunkhouse is set in tree lined surroundings and has private parking, a seating and barbeque area. It has a well equipped kitchen, a very comfortable lounge, a drying room, 2 toilets/showers and is well heated.

1.5 miles from Stornoway along the A857, second left past the hospital junction. From Harris take A859 for 40 miles, turn left at Stornoway roundabout onto the A857, then as above. Sleeps 16, with 4 family rooms. £9 to £10. Family rooms £32 to £36. Exclusive use £110 to £130.

Laxdale Holiday Park, 6 Laxdale Lane,
LAXDALE. Isle of Lewes HS2 0DR.
Contact: Gordon MacLeod
Tel: 01851 703234 Fax 01851 706966
gordon@laxdaleholidaypark.force9.co.uk

PEACEFUL LOCATION NEAR STORNOWAY, CHEAP COMFORTABLE MODERN FACILITIES

Wester Ross - Kyle of Lochalsh to Ullapool

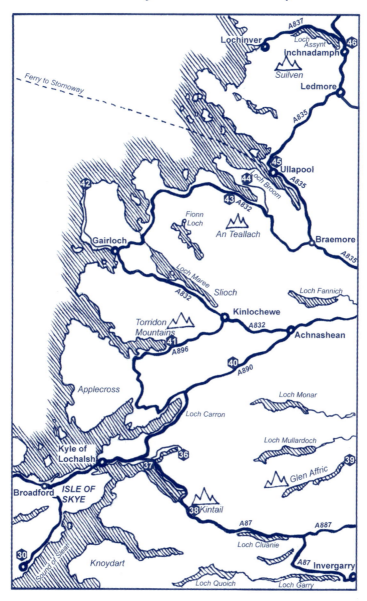

The West Coast between Kyle of Lochalsh and Ullapool includes some of the most spectacular coastal and mountain scenery in the Highlands, and some fantastic beaches. The approach to **Kyle of Lochalsh** from the Great Glen passes through Glensheil and past the Five sisters of Kintail – excellent hiking country with many Munros and extended mountain ridge walks.

A narrow single track road runs from Sheil Bridge out to **Glenelg** – a pretty village with views across to Skye and, in summer, a small ferry which carries up to 6 cars over the sea to Kylerhea on Skye. Just south of Glenelg the Iron Age Brochs are some of the best preserved in Scotland. A detour along this road also provides for the great views back to the Kintail mountains

Dun Telve Broch by Glenelg

By Dornie the famous **Eilean Donan Castle** stands on a peninsula at the head of Loch Duich. It has often been used in films and is frequently featured as an image of the Highlands in marketing promotions. The Castle is open to visitors in the summer months, and can be photographed at any time.

Kyle of Lochalsh was once the busy ferry port on the main route over to Skye – but the new bridge has changed this, and the village is now fairly quiet. A number of 'wildlife watching' boat trips are available from the harbour.

Travelling north on the coastal route from Kyle the road leads to the scenic village of **Plockton** – featured in the BBC tv series Hamish Macbeth. Continuing north along the southern shore of Loch Carron the road splits – inland to **Achnashellach** with its mountain & long distance walks, or back along the north shore of the Loch to Lochcarron village. The National Trust for Scotland owns the ruins of Strome Castle which overlooks the narrowest point of Loch Carron.

The narrow twisty road over to **Applecross** is one of the highest in Scotland, and the mountain pass offers fantastic views inland, and out over the sea to Skye & Rassay. Applecross itself is a scattering of houses around a stunning bay. The narrow road continues right around the coast – re-joining the main road just south of the village of Shieldaig.

The route continues along the southern shore of Upper Loch Torridon – with the dramatic **Torridon** mountains of Beinn Alligan & Liathac just to the north. **Torridon** offers many excellent low level and mountain walks – with some of the most striking mountain scenery in the north west. The mountains require that you are properly equipped, and ready for all weathers. There are many lower level walks – including a great coastal route from Diabeg to Redpoint. Much of the area around Torridon is owned and managed by the National Trust for Scotland. The NTS information point by Torridon village can provide details on the walks & trails. The eastern mountains fall within the **Beinn Eighe National Nature Reserve** – which is managed by Scottish Natural Heritage – there is a visitor centre with information on this reserve just north of Kinlochewe.

Gairloch is a popular holiday spot – with plenty to do for people or all ages and interests. Long sandy beaches, coastal trails, golf courses, sea-angling & wildlife spotting boat trips should be enough to keep anyone busy. The Heritage Museum provides an insight to the history of the local area.

The coastal route from Gairloch to Ullapool winds around a number of bays, the coastline dotted with numerous sandy beaches and rocky headlands. Just north of Poolewe are the internationally recognised Inverewe Gardens – run by the National Trust for Scotland. Open all year the gardens are best visited in the spring or summer, and include many rare sub-tropical plants that survive only because of the mild air resulting from the North Atlantic Drift

Gruinard Bay has a number of wonderful reddish sandy beaches around its length, but is best known for its island – scene of biological weapons experiments with anthrax during World War II. The island was cleared in the late 1980's but stands as a reminder of past events.

Dundonnell, on the shore of Little Loch Broom, is the starting point for the climb up to An Teallach – considered by many to be the finest peak in the north west, if not in the whole of Scotland. The climb requires a full day, and should only be attempted if you know what you are doing and have all the required equipment. There are great views back to the mountain from Badrallach on the northern shore of Little Loch Broom. (p42)

Just as the coastal route joins the Ullapool-Inverness road the NTS owned **Corrieshalloch Gorge** can be visited, and crossed on a slightly 'bouncy' suspension bridge – the view to the falls below is impressive, especially after heavy rain. Further towards **Ullapool** it is worth stopping at **Leckmelm Gardens** – where a variety of unusual trees & plants can be seen – in a much more informal setting than at the much larger gardens at Inverewe

Ullapool is the main village on the west coast north of Kyle of Lochalsh and has a full range of shops & tourists services. It is also of course the departure point for ferries to Stornoway on the Western Isles. There are numerous places to eat and a fair number of pubs – some on the seafront with views down Loch Broom.

Ullapool is also a good base from which to explore the mountains just to the south around Ben Wyvis, and also the Coigach mountains to the north. There are also numerous lower level and coastal walks nearby. From the harbour there are boat trips to the Summer Isles - ideal for wildlife watchers – and sea fishing trips can be arranged. The Ullapool Museum is worth a visit – with plenty of displays on the local history of the Loch Broom area. The leisure centre has a pool & a sauna – so there are things to enjoy even if it were to rain!

West Coast Public Transport

Unfortunately there is no regular direct public transport that follows the coastline. There are however various options that do exist, and by using postbuses and other local services it is possible to reach even the most remote of locations.

There is a regular train service from Inverness to Kyle of Lochalsh (via Garve, 3 times a day Mon to Sat), and a regular bus service via Loch Ness & Glen Sheil. The train north from Kyle follows the coast, passing Plockton & the southern shore of Loch Carron. From Strathcarron station post bus services operate on the route up to Torridon, and around the coast from Sheldaig to Applecross (There are no buses direct to Applecross over the high pass). Continue on the train for Achnasheallach, Achnashean & Garve. From Torridon a postbus also operates to Kinlochewe and Achnashean station. From there the 3 times a week (Mon, Wed, Sat) Westerbus (tel 01445 712255) service from Inverness to Gairloch

From Gairloch there is a postbus service out to Melvaig (to the end of the road to Rua Reidh lighthouse). Westerbus operate a daily service around the coast via Poolewe, to Laide, which continues via Gruinard Bay & Dundonnell to Inverness on 3 days (Mon, Wed, Sat).

There are frequent buses (with Citylink, Rapsons and others) from Inverness to/from Ullapool (via Garve) and these usually meet the CalMac Ferry from Ullapool to Stornoway. There are daily services from Ullapool to Lochinver, and in the summer there is a daily service from Inverness to Durness on the north coast, which passes Garve, Ullapool & Lochinver. These services operate on the same route's if you are travelling from north to south.

There are no bus services on Sundays.

Car Hire is available in Ullapool from the Filling Station (01854 612298) and from Daley's deals (01854 612848).
Mountain Bike hire is available from the Ullapool Tourist Hostel (p57)

36. Tigh Iseabail Bunkhouse

Croft cottage converted to warm comfortable Hostel. Both bedrooms have en-suite toilet and showers. Central heated throughout by oil stove. Gas hob and microwave. Laundry facilities in adjacent drying shed. Bike hire free for 2 nights stay. Transport to hostel can be arranged. Games room. Visit Glomach waterfall (U.K.'s highest). Gaelic speaking owner.
From north turn left onto A87. 4km turn off left at sign to Camushuinie Sallachy Killilan. From east on A87 1km past Eilean Donan Castle turn right. Hostel at Camusluinie road end.OS 33, NG 947284
Sleeps 6, 4 in bunks, 2 in Double Rm. £7.50
Breakfast from £8.50 (self catering)

Whitefalls', 1 Camuslunie, Killilan,
Kyle IV40 8EA..
Contact: Willie or Sheena
Tel/Fax: 01599 588205

BREAKFAST OF FRESH ORGANIC EGGS INCLUDED

37. Silver Fir Bunkhouse

This cosey, comfortable, wood-lined bunkhouse is set alongside our house in a big child friendly organic garden. There are sea views and a wood burning stove. Free tea and coffe is provided and guests are invited to help themselves to herbs from the garden. There is a shop and post office in the village nearby (1km) together with excellent leisure facilities including Eilean Donan Castle, a craft shop, poney trekking and three pubs.
Turn off the A87 at Dornie. Turn right at the T-junction in the village. Follow the road along the loch for about 1km until you come to the fence. That's us.
Open all year. No of beds 4 £10 per person

Carndubh, Dornie
By Kyle of Lochalsh
South West Rossshire. IV40 8EP
Tel 01559 555264
Mobile: 07786 675118

38. Morvich Kintail NTS Hostel

Fully refurbished in 2001. Provides high quality accommodation, well fitted kitchen, dining room, common room, modern showers/toilets, drying room, Laundry room. Separate self contained family room.

OS 33, GR 968210. 2km from A87, 25km before Kyle of Lochalsh.
Sleeps 24 in bunks. One 4 person family room.
Group rate for whole hostel £165 per night.
Individuals £7.50 per person per night.

Booking essential.

Morvich, Kintail, By Kyle of Lochalsh, Wester Ross IV40 8HQ
Contact Lisa Mackay
(NTS Central Booking) 0131 243 9331
E-mail: lmackay@nts.org.uk
Web: www.nts.org.uk

WONDERFUL MOUNTAIN SETTING, OVER 40 MUNRO'S WITHIN 30KM.

39. Cougie Lodge

Cosy cabin with wood stove for heating. Sleeps 5 or 6 in three bedrooms. Sitting/diningroom. Kitchen, Bathroom with toilet + small 2nd kitchen. Basic facilities. Electricity for lighting only (generator no mains). Gas for cooking and hot water.

A831 to Cannich, continue to Tomich follow F.E. sign at end of village to Plodda Falls go past car park uphill follow signs to Cougie. NH242 212

Cougie Lodge
Cougie, Tomich, Strathglass
Beauly, Inverness-shire
IV4 7LY
Email: pete@knckfin.com

PEACEFUL LOCATION, STUNNING SCENERY AND WARM FRIENDLY WELCOME

40. Gerry's Hostel

20 peaks over 2,500ft. Low level walks by strath and glen. Centre for Geology, Botany, Ornithology, cycling, golfing. Petanque and relaxing. Cottage comforts, log fire, wildlife. 'Lord of the Rings' type neighbourhood. On most scenic railway in Britain. Real ale & good food at local pub.

A890 50 miles west of Inverness, at Achnashellach, on the Kyle railway line.
OS 25, GR 037493
Sleeps 20 in bunkbeds/family rooms.
From £10 to £11.

Craig, Achnashellach, Strathcarron, Wester Ross IV54 8YU.
Contact: Gerry Howkins
Tel: 01520 766232
gerryshostel@freedomland.co.uk

WALKING - CLIMBING - HOT SHOWERS - DRYING ROOM - NON-SMOKERS.

41. Mol Mor – Torridon

High quality basic accommodation with 3 bedrooms, common room/kitchen, drying room with laundry facilities, two shower rooms, fridge/freezers. Wood burning stove & central heating. Has to be seen to be appreciated. Ideal location for exploring a wonderful mountain area.

OS24, GR898556. 60 miles west of Inverness, 800m from the junction of the A896 and Diabaig Road. Sleeps 10 in bunkbeds
GROUP BOOKINGS ONLY
£65 per night or £325 per week for whole hostel.

Mol Mor, The Mains, Torridon, By Achnasheen, Wester Ross, IV22 2EZ
Contact Lisa Mackay
(NTS Central Booking) 0131 243 9331
E-mail: lmackay@nts.org.uk
Web: www.nts.org.uk

PEACEFUL CONVERTED STEADING AT HEAD OF LOCH TORRIDON.

42. Rua Reidh Lighthouse

From Gairloch take the minor road signposted to Melvaig and follow this for 12 miles to the lighthouse. OS 19, GR 740919
Hot showers. Dinner and breakfast available if booked in advance. Open all year except the 4 weeks after New Year.
Sleeps 20 - 14 in three bunk rooms, and 6 in twin/double rooms. £8.50 to £16.00 Breakfast available £4.50.
Contact: Fran or Chris
Tel/Fax: 01445 771263
E-mail: ruareidh@netcomuk.co.uk
Web:www.ruareidh.co.uk

Melvaig, Gairloch, Ross-shire
IV21 2EA.

Dramatic, remote location. Comfortable, warm & homely accommodation. Hot showers. Dinner and breakfast available if booked in advance. Open all year except the 4 weeks after New Year.

There is also plenty to offer to those interested in history. From mesolithic caves to Bronze and Iron age hut circles, medieval forts to fortified islands, the local area is rich in archaelogical remains. Past struggles to make a living from this inhospitable land are also much in evidence with abandoned crofting hamlets and pastures left to return to heathland.

The moors behind the lighthouse are home to a wealth of seabirds, wading birds, flora and fauna. There are a couple of deserted sandy beaches an hour's walk away which make a wonderful excursion, or, for those who don't want to walk as far, a saunter along the cliffs gives breathtaking views of the birds nesting on magnificent sea stacks.

Gairloch itself is an attractive small town with several hotels, coffee shops, museum, a variety of activities, shops, etc. The famous Inverewe Gardens are 4 miles and well worth a visit.

DRAMATIC, REMOTE LOCATION. COMFORTABLE, WARM & HOMELY ACCOMMODATION

43. Sail Mhor Croft Hostel (V)

Welcome to Sail Mhor Croft, the hostel we established in 1978. Nestling below the famous 'An Teallach' mountain range, we are perfectly located for walking some of Scotland's finest mountains, to visit our beautiful local beaches, or to just enjoy the peace and tranquillity of the area. The hostel which stands in 1/2 an acre of garden offers central heating, excellent showers, drying room and lounge. Meals available.
On A832 midway between Ullapool & Gairloch - 1.5 miles (2km) west of Dundonnell Hotel. Westerbus from Inverness on Mon, Wed, Sat only. OS 19 GR GH064 893. Sleeps 16 in bunkbeds. £9. Breakfast available £3.50.

Camusnagaul, Dundonnell,
Ross-shire, IV23 2QT
Contact: Dave or Lynda
Tel/Fax: 01854 633224
E-mail: sailmhor@btopenworld.com
Web: www.sailmhor.co.uk

FRIENDLY ACCOMMODATION. RURAL SETTING. MOUNTAINS - SCENERY.

44. Badrallach Bothy & Camp Site (V)

On the tranquil shores of Little Loch Broom, overlooking the mighty An Teallach, here you can walk in the wilderness, view abundant flora – orchids, saxifroges – watch golden eagles, otters, porpoises, seals & deer, or enjoy good company and a tune in the bothy by the peat stove under gas lighting. Hot showers and B&B/cottage available fore more luxury.
Turn off A832 1 mile east of Dundonnell Hotel, Take single track road 7 miles to Badrallach. Westerbus stops at road end Mon/Wed/Sat . Ullapool to Altnaharrie foot ferry in summer. OS 19, GR 065915
Sleeps 12 on Alpine platforms. £4.00 to £5.50

Croft 9, Badrallach, Dundonnell,
Ross-shire, IV23 2QP
Contact: Mick or Ali Stott,
Tel:01854 633281
E-mail: michael.stott2@virgin.net
www.badrallach.com

LOCHSHORE, AN TEALLACH, A DRAM, GAS LIGHTS, PEAT FIRE, BLISS.

45. Ullapool Tourist Hostel (V)

Superb homely hostel with full central heating & multifuel stove in comfortable lounge with TV, video and CD player. Drying room with dehumidifier & heater. Excellent kitchen with 2 hobs & cooker, Rayburn & dishwasher, freezer & fridge. Laundry. Separate dining room. Internet access £1 / hour. Free tea & coffee.
Bike hire available

Regular bus service from Inverness (buses run to meet Stornoway ferry). By car- from Inverness cross the Kessock bridge, and follow signs for Ullapool on the A835.
Sleeps 22 in bunks, with 5 family rooms (some en-suite) Twin rooms can be arranged. Bed only £9.25. Breakfast avail. £2.

West House, West Argyle Street,
Ullapool, Ross-shire, IV26 2TY
Contact: Richard / Andy
Tel/Fax: 01854 613126.
r.lindsay@btinternet.com
www.scotpackers-hostels.co.uk

HOMELY FRIENDLY HOSTEL WITH SUPERB FACILITIES.

The North – Sutherland, Caithness

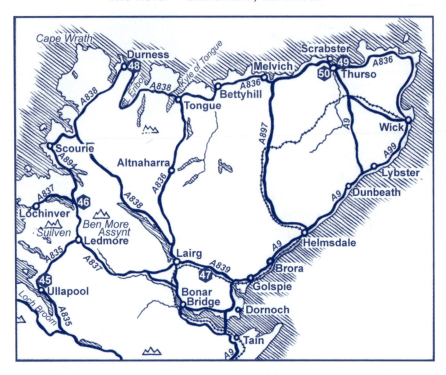

To the north of Ullapool the dramatic mountain scenery of **Inverpolly & Assynt** unfolds. Isolated mountains rise up from an undulating landscape of lochs, lochans and rocky knolls. The coastline includes a mixture of secluded sandy beaches, rocky inlets and towering sandstone cliffs. Scattered communities are concentrated along the coast from Achiltibue to **Lochinver** (the main village – Tourist Office & Visitor Centre) and around the coast to Kylesku via Stoer & Drumbeg. Inland the settlements of Elphin & Inchnadamph represent what were once more populated townships. The Assynt mountains (Ben More Assynt & Conival (both Munros), Quinag, Suilven & Canisp), are popular with hillwalkers & climbers, and the lochs and rivers are a draw to anglers. The varied habitats and rocks of Assynt make the area popular with wildlife enthusiasts, geologists and botanists.

The ruins of **Ardvreck Castle** (above) and Calda House on the shores of Loch Assynt are reminders of a troubled past, dominated by clan rivalries.

North of **Kylesku** the dramatic scenery continues all the way to Durness. Off the coast from Scourie the bird reserve at Handa Island is a prime site for breeding seabirds, and further north a long walk to **Sandwood Bay** leads to an isolated sandy beach over a mile long. To reach Cape Wrath – the most north westerly point on the mainland – you must take a ferry & minibus from beside the **Cape Wrath** Hotel, a few miles south of Durness.

Smoo Cave, the Craft village & the extensive sandy beaches are the main attractions of Durness – plus one of the most northerly Golf courses in the UK. The spectacular mountain scenery (including Ben Hope by Tongue – the most northerly Munro) and dramatic coastline continue along the north coast to **Bettyhill**. Here the Invernaver nature reserve and the Strathnaver Museum are both worth a visit. At **Melvich** the landscape levels out as the farmlands of Caithness are reached to the east, and to the south are the peatlands of the 'Flow Country', and the RSPB reserve at Forsinard.

Thurso is the the most northerly town on the mainland, and also the largest on the north coast. Renowned for the nuclear power plant at Dounreay (yes – it has a visitor centre!), Thurso is also a popular base for surfers (although the water is cold the surf is excellent!) and is the stopping point for car ferries to Orkney & Shetland.

To the east of Thurso is **Dunnet Head** – the most northerly point of the mainland. It offers great views north to Orkney on a clear day from the lighthouse on the point. This, along with **Duncansby Head** and its associated sea stacks, are far greater attractions than better known **John O'Groats** – which is not much more than a Hotel, a tourist office and craft shops. Fortunately there is also a passenger ferry to Orkney. Half way between Dunnet Head & Duncasby Head is the Castle of Mey – a former home of the late Queen Elizabeth the Queen Mother. It opened to the public for the first time in Summer 2002.

The coastline south towards Inverness is less dramatic than the west coast, but boasts its own charm. Just north of Wick are the cliff top ruins of the Sinclair and Girnigoe Castles. In Wick the Caithness Glass Visitor Centre & Wick Heritage Centre are worth a visit. South of Wick near Lybster there are prehistoric burial chambers which rival those on Orkney. The Dunbeath Heritage Centre, and the **Timespan Heritage Centre at Helmsdale** offer an excellent guide to the history of the Northern Highlands.

Dunrobin Castle, just outside **Golspie**, was the seat of the Duke of Sutherland, and is one of the largest houses in the Highlands with great gardens reaching down to the sea. It is open April to October. **Dornoch** is now famous as the site of Madonna's recent wedding, but also boasts some great architecture, fine beaches and fine golf course.

Travel & Transport in the North

On the west coast there are year round bus services north from Ullapool, but only as far as Lochinver & Drumbeg. In summer (May to Oct) there is a once daily return service from Inverness all the way to Durness, via Ullapool & Lochinver. There is fortunately a reasonable network of postbuses – from Ullapool these will take you out to Achiltibue. From Lochinver the postbuses run North as far as Scourie, and east to Lairg - itself a hub for postbus services to Durness & Tongue on the north coast.

Lairg is also a link to the main Inverness to Wick/Thurso 'North Highland' rail line – allowing connections to Rogart, Golspie and the east coast, and passing through some great coastal & inland scenery on the route to Thurso.
There are many bus services on the A9 route from Inverness to Thurso/Wick, but only a summer service along the north coast between Durness & Thurso.

A private car can make it easier to get around in the north – if you have not hired a car with easycar or other national provider then local Car Hire is available in Ullapool (01851 706622), Thurso (01847 893101/894946), Wick (01955 502103/604125 & Brora (01408 621356) Cycling is another great way to explore the north - Cycle Hire is available in Ullapool (01854 613126), Brora (01408 621658), Thurso (01847 895385) & Wick (01955 603636) – be sure to reserve space in advance if you wish to take a cycle on the North Highland rail line for some sections.

Walking, Hiking & Climbing in Caithness & Sutherland.

The north is an excellent destination for those seeking to enjoy great walks of all varieties amid spectacular scenery – with the bonus that if you can avoid the peak season it is an area where you can still often have the hill to yourself.

One of the most popular hikes in the area is to climb to the craggy summit of Stac Pollaidh – often referred to as 'Scotland's Miniature Mountain' – at the heart of the Inverpolly National Nature Reserve, just north of Ullapool. Other hills in the area – Ben Mor Coigach, Cul Mor, Cul Beag and the Assynt mountains (**Ben More Assynt & Conival** (both Munros), Quinag, Suilven & Canisp, provide enough challenges to keep a keen hillwalker occupied for a week or so.

There are also numerous lower level walks in the area – including the full day hike from Lochinver to Elphin, passing below and between Suilven & Canisp, a 6hr circular route from Inchnadamph to Eas Coul Aluin waterfall (the UK's tallset), walks up the limestone valleys near the Inchnadamph 'Bone Caves', and the coastal path from Stoer Lighthouse to Stoer Point & the Old Man of Stoer sea stack.

Further to the north the mountains of Ben Stack, Arkle, Foinaven and Scotland's most northerly Munro of **Ben Hope** all stand as isolated peaks in one of the last true wilderness areas in Europe. There are also opportunities for lower level walks to such places as Sandwood Bay – a mile long beach of pure sand – with cliffs and sea stacks at the ends. It is possible to continue north along the coast to Cape Wrath, and then along the service track to the summer only ferry over the Kyle of Durness (but check the MoD are not using the firing range when you plan your hike!)
The northern section of the **Cape Wrath Trail** (a 200 mile route from Ft William to Cape wrath) passes right through this area from Ben More Assynt to the Cape – and provides a very challenging long distance route.

To the east the last of the 'big' hills are **Ben Loyal** & the munro of **Ben Kilbreck** – both providing stunning views north and west over the 'flow country' to the Orkney Isles in the distance. Elsewhere there are many coastal walks around Bettyhill, Melvich and the **Caithness Coastal Walk** between Duncasby Head and John O'Groats – passing some high cliffs well populated with seabirds during the breeding season. A short walk up any of the lower hills of western Caithness will also provide views across the peatlands and farmed areas of the north east. Elsewhere in east Sutherland there are a number of forest trails – some suitable for cycling as well as walking – details of these from Forest Enterprise in Dornoch – 01862 810359, www.forestry.gov.uk.

Rock Climbing In Caithness & Sutherland

While there are some recognised routes on the sandstone mountains – notably Ben Mor Coigach, Stack Pollaidh & Suilven – the majority of the climbing routes in the north are concentrated around the coast, at Reiff (near Achiltibue) or on some of the seas stacks at Stoer & elsewhere.

Guided Walking & Climbing in Caithness

The northern hills & mountains are often more remote and less well visited than some of the southern peaks – please always take a good map, a compass (& know how to use them!) and even in summer expect the weather to be changeable. If you wish the security of a guide then consider contacting Cape Adventures (01971 521006) . For longer walking holidays in the area try Walkabout Scotland, Lomond Walking Holidays, North West Frontiers or C-N-Do Scotland – all of whom offer week long trips to the area.

Canoe Sport in Caithness & Sutherland

The Northern Highlands include an extreme diversity of paddling opportunities. So much so that it is difficult to give a concise over view of what is realistically on offer – on inland lochs, white water rivers, surfing beaches, long sea kayaking journeys.

There is a very long, indented coastline – with sandy beaches in parts – towering cliffs in others – and plenty of islands to explore. During the long summer days there is a wealth of coastal hopping to do by sea kayak – but always check the weather and the tides locally.

Sea Kayaking. In the north & east area there are more local sea trips to explore the East Coast between Lybster and Helmsdale; visits to the islands in the Kyle of Tongue; and to the west explore the Summer Isles from Achiltibuie. Unless you are very experienced it is best to go with someone who knows the area - the tides here are notorious.

River Kayaking. All the local Caithness rivers are really spate rivers and require sufficient water and are fairly technical. Water levels are most likely to be suitable in the autumn/winter but may rise fast at any time. Paddling is mainly concentrated on the rivers Thurso, Helmsdale, Brora, Carron, Findhorn – keep clear of fishermen!

Inland Lochs. Loch Shin, Naver, Loyal, Rinisadale all offer the opportunity to make fairly extended trips on open inland water

Surf Kayaking. Caithness – mainly around Thurso, the northern coast and Wick - has some of the best surfing breaks in the world. World Kayak Championships have been routinely held here. The local Pentland Canoe Club will introduce beginners to the sport if contacted before hand.

Equipment Hire, Paddlesport courses, coaching & guided trips

If you are not touring the north with your kyak / canoe – never fear – equipment can be hired & even guided trips can be arranged!

Thurso Surf School – Spittal, Caithness – Approved Surf School – Tel 01847 841300
Cape Adventure – Rhiconich, By Lairg – Surfing, Sea Kayaking – Tel 01971 521006
Kyle Adventures – Bonar Bridge – canoe hire & guided trips - Tel 01863 766691

Cycling and Mountain Biking in Caithness, Sutherland and Ross-shire.

Cycling & Mountain Biking in the vast area to the north and west of Inverness probably offers the widest range of biking challenges than anywhere else in Scotland. There are some "organised" waymarked trails in forests – look out for the Forest Enterprise leaflet in Tourist Offices – and also the opportunity to travel long distances on quiet single track roads. In summer a ferry service (departs from by Cape Wrath Hotel) will take cyclists over the Kyle of Durness from where a 12 mile track leads to the dramatic Cape Wrath lighthouse – perched at the top of some of the highest sea cliffs in the UK. In other areas there are few organised off-road tracks – so please check with landowners before heading into the hills on two wheels.

Bike hire is available in many areas – and most of these establishments will also be able to assist with spare parts and servicing. Remember there are no suppliers around the coast from Ullapool until Thurso – so take some spares with you! Reservations are essential if you wish to take a bike on the Inverness to Wick/Thurso train line.

Bicycle Bothy,	Brora	Tel 01408 621658
Bike & camping Shop,	Thurso	Tel 01847 896124
Leisure Activites,	Thurso	Tel 01847 895385
Wheels Cycle Shop,	Wick	Tel 01955603636
Fairburn Activity Centre,	Muir of Ord	Tel 01997 433397
ScotpackersBike Hire,	Ullapool	Tel 01854 613126

46. Inchnadamph Lodge (V)

25 miles north of Ullapool on the main road to Lochinver / Durness – at the east end of Loch Assynt, next to Inchnadamph Hotel. 12 miles east of Lochinver. OS 15, GR 253218.
Public Transport. Year round there is regular public transport to our door from Ullapool, Lochinver and Lairg (for trains to/from Inverness & Thurso/Wick). In the summer there is also a daily direct service to /from Inverness and Durness.

Sleeps 34 in bunkbeds in rooms sleeping 4 to 8 people, plus 6 twin/dbl/family rooms.
Bunks £10.95, Twin/Dbls £16.95 pppn.
BREAKFAST INCLUDED FOR ALL.

Inchnadamph Lodge, Loch Assynt,
Nr Lochinver, Sutherland IV27 4HL.
Contact: Chris Tel: 01571 822218
E-mail: hostel@inch-lodge.co.uk
Web: www.inch-lodge.co.uk

We offer warm comfortable hostel style dormitory rooms and private twin or double rooms in a former highland shooting lodge. Facilities include a well equipped self-catering kitchen, a large dining room (seats 40+), excellent hot powerful showers, a big drying room, full laundry facilities and real fires in lounge and dining room.

A separate TV lounge with Hi-Fi etc is located in our annex – well away from the sleeping accommodation – keeping any late night noise to a minimum! On-site shop & off-licence for basic provisions, beer & wine.

An ideal base for walkers, climbers, families and backpackers from which to explore the beautiful mountains, wildlife, history and coastline of Assynt. We are right at the foot of Sutherland's higest mountain – Ben more Assynt – and just a short walk from shores of Loch Assynt – not far from the ruins of Ardvreck Castle.

Fantastic sandy beaches are just a short drive away at Achmelvich or Clachtoll.

Bar Meals available at the Inchnadamph Hotel next door.

QUALITY ACCOMMODATION AMID SPECTACULAR MOUNTAIN SCENERY

47. sleeperzzz.com

The carriages are at Rogart Railway Station, a small crofting community in beautiful Strath Fleet with a shop, pub and post office. Visit Dunrobin Castle, see salmon at Lairg, sample whisky at Glenmorangie, or just unwind amid stunning scenery. Facilities include showers, s/c kitchen, private compartments sleeping two, and free bikes. 10% reduction for rail users and cyclists. Pub/restaurant nearby

At railway station in centre of village, 4 miles from A9. on A839 3 trains daily in each direction on Inverness – Wick route. OS 16, GR 725019. Sleeps 20 in 2 bed compartments. £9. Breakfast available £2.50.

Rogart Station, Rogart,
Sutherland, IV28 3XA
Contact: Kate Roach
Tel/Fax: 01408 641343
E-mail: kate@sleeperzzz.com

STAY ON A FIRST CLASS TRAIN

48. The Lazy Crofter Bunkhouse

The Lazy Crofter is a small independent hostel set amongst powerful mountain and coastal scenery in Durness, northwest Highlands of Scotland. We offer quality self-catering accommodation to groups, families and individuals at unbeatable prices. A perfect base for walkers, cyclists, geologists, archaeologists and wildlife enthusiasts.

Durness is about 2.5 hours drive north of Inverness. Public transport is available 6 days a week by train to Lairg & then postbus. During summer a direct bus operates daily from Inverness.

OS 9, GR NC406679

Sleeps 20 in Bunks, 2 twin rooms. £9.00

The Lazy Crofter, Durine, Durness,
Sutherland, IV27 4PN
Contact: Fiona / Robbie,
Tel: 01971 511 202/366 Fx 01971
511321 fiona@durnesshostel.com
www.durnesshostel.com

SMALL HIGHLAND HOSTEL, BIG HIGHLAND HOSPITALITY.

49. Thurso Youth Club Hostel (V)

Occupying a converted watermill that overlooks the river and park, we provide an excellent base for exploring the area or stopover for travel connections. All local amenities within 5 minutes walk. Comfortable accommodation with a friendly atmosphere. Well-equipped kitchen, dining area, games rooms and TV/Video lounge. No curfew. Price includes showers, bed linen and continental breakfast.

Millbank Road is on the south side of Thurso River and runs parallel to it. From railway station – turn right down Lover's Lane, enter the park and cross over the footbridge. Sleeps 22 in bunkbeds - £8 including breakfast.

Old Mill, Millbank Road,
Thurso, Caithness, KW14 8PS
Contact: Allan Hourston
Tel/Fax: 01847 892964.
t.y.c.hostel@btinternet.com
www.tyc-hostel.com

THURSO'S ONLY 'VISITSCOTLAND' GRADED HOSTEL. EXCELLENT VALUE

The North – Caithness, Sutherland

50. Sandra's Backpackers (V)

In town centre 200m from train station, 50m from bus stop, Taxi rank outside the door and free transport to Scrabster for the 12 noon ferry to Orkney.
Sleeps Aprox 30 people in twin double family and dorm rooms. Price: £9 per person including bedding and breakfast pack.
Twin Double room £28 Family room £34
10% discount on all food from Sandra's snack bar
Contact: George, Sandra or James Carson
Tel: 01847 894575
Sandras-backpackers@ukf.net
www.sandras-backpackers.ukf.net

24-26 Princes Street,
THURSO, KW14 7BQ.

Thurso's principal hostel located in the centre of the most northerly mainland town in Scotland. An ideal base for touring the north coast or for leaving or returning from Orkney. Although only four years old the hostel this year is being extended and refurbished to nearly double the size with a new full self catering kitchen and common room, laundry and drying room. All rooms have en-suite facilities and are centrally heated with piping hot showers. Accesses to the internet and bike hire are available on the premises. There is a snack bar down stairs where if you are feeling lazy they will be happy to serve you a hearty breakfast, midday snack or evening meal.
Recommended by Lonely planet, Lets go and Rough guide
This hostel is one of the many highland hostels. Run by a family with lots of backpacking experience.

FRIENDLY CLEAN AND COMFORTABLE. CENTRAL SNACK-BAR. ALL FACILITIES.

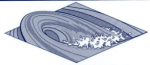

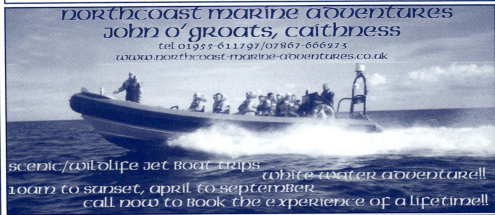

Thurso Taxi - John O' Groats Ferries

Set sail for The Orkney Isle

£24.00 Return Off peak fare

John o' Groats to Kirkwell

Cross to Orkney any morning -return any afternoon

www.jogferry.co.uk

01955 611353

Free Taxi

7.45 Am
Thurso -Jog Ferry
£3.50 Single p/p
£6.50 Return p/p

Please book in advance for 7.45 Am Taxi

01847 811555

Wnen using the above services why not stay at
Sandra's Backpackers Hostel
01847 894575
Either before going or on your return

The North – Caithness, Sutherland

The Orkney Islands

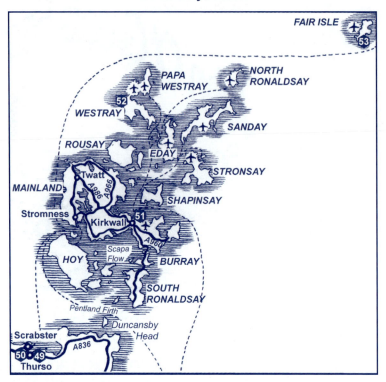

Orkney lies off the north coast, a collection of islands offering freedom and wide open spaces in which past and present live side by side and where many of the dwellings, lifestyles and customs of its earliest inhabitants have been carefully conserved for all to enjoy. The two main towns in mainland Orkney are Stromness and the capital, Kirkwall. Orkney caters for walkers, bird watchers and has excellent diving facilities at Scapa Flow. Orkneys history stems from the Neolithic age to World War 1 and World War 2 through to the present day.

Places of interest, some dating from 5,000 years ago, are Cuween Cairn, Maeshowe, Standing Stones of Stenness, Ring of Brodgar, Skara Brae, Broch of Gurness, Earls Palace, Brough of Birsay and Kirbister Farm - plus many other different sites of interest such as the Italian Chapel and St. Magnus Cathedral in Kirkwall. All the outlying islands off the mainland of Orkney are accessible by different ferries. Each island has its own characteristics from beautiful sandy beaches, cliffs, tranquility and scenery. **Westray** is the largest of the 'north islands' of Orkney, with a population of around 700. The island has farmland, moorland, spectacular cliffs & sandy beaches. The cliffs at Noup Head form part of an RSPB reserve - a vast seabird colony in the breeding season. In the main settlement of Pierowall there is a Heritage Centre, and the ruins of Notland Castle.

Midway between Orkney & Shetland is **Fair Isle** – a mere 3 miles long by 1.5 miles wide the island has a population of about 70. The island is popular with naturalists – being on a regular migration path for birds, and also home to a wide variety of flowering plants. The cliffs on the north coast are particularly spectacular.

Orkney Transport

By Air
Flights to Kirkwall from Inverness, Aberdeen, Glasgow and Edinburgh are operated by British Airways. These can be busy in the summer so book ahead.

By Ferry
Northlink Ferries operate a car ferry to Stromness from Scrabster (Thurso) and Aberdeen. In the summer months there is a passenger only ferry from John 'O' Groats to Burnwich (S.Ronaldsay). Coach Services from Inverness meet with the ferries in Scrabster, or travel in by train to Thurso and then bus to Scrabster.

Events & Festivals
22-25th May 2003   Orkney Folk Festival – various locations
31st May 2003 at 03.45   partial Eclipse of the moon by the sun to create a ring
1st January 2004 The Ba' Games – Men & Boys – Uppies V Downies – Kirkwall

Walking and Climbing in Orkney
Orkney does not have difficult walking country, which is high or mountainous – but walking routes can still be classed as strenuous. Routes are always interesting through spectacular scenery along the coasts or over inland hills and moorland. There are no inland crags for climbing, however coastal sandstone cliffs are truly awesome!

It is always advisable to let someone know where you are planning to go walking and when you intend to return. Walking boots are always advised along with adequate weatherproof clothing with food and drink for the day in remoter areas. Always take care on high coastal cliff paths. Most walks will have a specific route of interest, passed ancient archaeological sites, sea bird colonies, wildlife and ecology, geo (blow) holes, or whales playing at specific times of the year.

Orkney Walks
Try the walk from Armadale to Port Mor – along the steep rocky shore to Cathedral Rock - where seabirds nest along the cliffs – along to the large steep sided bay of Port Mor – with caves and arches – where fulmars, shags and eider ducks nest on the outer skerries or walk the Borsa Island route along massive sea cliffs, passed the blow hole and sea bird colonies with views of Cape Wrath in the distance. Or take the car/passenger ferry from Kirkwall to Eday Island to visit the heritage site. On the Isle of Stronsay walk the Odin Bay path to the magnificent arch at the Vat of Kirkbuster past ancient broch remains and sea stacks.

Sea Stack Climbing in Orkney. A large proportion of the climbing in these islands is virgin and unexplored – many recognised rock routes have only had a few ascents. This means that there is an enormous potential for new routes. The island of Hoy off Radwick and around Yesnaby Castle (Mainland) is the location with most established routes. The Old Man of Hoy can become very busy in summer. The famous **Needle** is a big adventure also off south Radwick. On S Ronaldsay is **Stackabank** with at least one serious route, which is not often climbed; along with the little known Clett of Crura on the East Coast of the island. West Mainland has the spectacular, remote cliffs of North Gaulton Castle which are little visited. Also on West Mainland Yesanby Castle where a spectacular sea stack and local cliffs have a large number of established routes. To the north is the small and remote Stack O'Roo sea stack, which is not often visited. Off the northern most tip of mainland Orkney is Standard Rock. The island of Westray has a small stack at Castle of Burrian.

Many of the routes are in the upper end of difficulty and are not for beginners.

Cycling in Orkney

These islands are excellent cycling country with quiet roads, gently rolling hills and easy countryside to travel through. Away from the main roads there is a whole network of small country roads, which link small communities. Bikes are also an excellent way to get to some of the remoter sea cliffs for climbing.

Travelling by cycle is a really convenient way to visit many of the archaeological and wildlife sites in the islands. Some pre-planning and homework with a ferry timetable is a good way to make the most of your cycle tour.

Try the 19 miles Birsay – Stromess route through to Kirkwall - on to the 5000 year old Maeshow burial site – passed the Ring of Brodgar – then visit the ancient site of Skara Brae near the Bay of Skiall – then north on to Birsay. For a really long route, Orkney is a link in the 1242km Scotland section of North Sea Cycle Route.

Cycle Hire.

Bikes on Hoy	Whaness	Tel 01856 791225
Stromness Cycle Hire	Stromness	Tel 01856 850750
Orkney Cycle Hire	Stromness	Tel 01856 850255
Bobby's Bike Hire	Kirkwall	Tel 01856 875777

Sea Kayaking in Orkney

The coastline here is a wide mix of long sandy beaches to high sandstone cliffs, arches and stacks. The islands outside Mainland Orkney all have tiny harbours where food can be re-stocked. These islands are mainly for more experienced sea kayakers who have brought their own gear with them. While Orkney is only a short distance off the Scottish Mainland's north coast, the notorious currents of the Pentland Firth make this crossing a serious undertaking unless the weather and tides are right – as well as having adequate previous experience.

51. Kirkwall Peedie Hostel

Over looking the sea in Kirkwall, main town of Orkney, Peedie hostel can accommodate 8 people in 3 rooms. The hostel is 2 minutes from the town centre and 5 minutes to ferries to other islands. Pubs, hotels, bike hire, car hire, restaurants & take-aways, and sports centre all within 5 mins walk. Open all year – No curfew, All day access.

No 1 Ayre Houses, Ayre Road, Kirkwall, Orkney, KW15 1QX
Contact: Cath Swanney
Tel: 01856 875477.
E-mail:
kirkwallpeediehostel@talk21.com

Sleeps 8, in 2 twin rooms and 1 family room of 4.

£10.00

PRE-BOOKED GROUPS ONLY. FLEXIBLE FRIENDLY AND FANTASTIC FUN.

52. Bisgeos Backpackers Hostel

Traditional bothy style hostel, re-built to an exceptional standard. Flagstone/timber floors, nets, ropes & fishboxes! Contrasted with modern appliances, under floor heating & top quality fixtures & fittings.Situated above Westray's western cliffs commanding a breathtaking view of Rousay, Orkney mainland & Hoy silhouetted on the southern horizon.

Minibus available from the Ferry Terminal. The Bisgeos Hostel is signposted from Pierwall Village.
Sleeps 12 in 2*4 bed rooms and 2* 2 bed rooms.
£8 to £10

Bisgeos Hostel & Cottages, Isle of Westray, Orkney, KW17 2DW
Contact: Alena
Tel/Fax: 01857 677420
www.bis-geos.co.uk e-mail via website

SMALL FRIENDLY STRESSLESS COZY HOSTEL WITH SPECTACULAR VIEWS

53. The Puffin - Fair Isle Hostel

A converted Fish Store provides basic but comfortable accommodation on a wonderful island, often described as one of the remotest communities in the UK. Common room, dining & kitchen, 2 bedrooms, showers & toilets

Located on the south haven of Fair Isle. Travel by boat or plane from Shetland.
Sleeps 12 in bunkbeds.
Group rate for hostel £200 per week.
Individuals £5 per person per night (Students £3).

The Puffin Hostel, Fair Isle, Shetland, ZE2
Contact: Bob Elliot
Tel: 01463 732627 Fax 01463 732620
E-mail:belliot@nts.org.uk

BEAUTIFUL LOCATION ON A BEAUTIFUL ISLAND.

The Shetland Isles

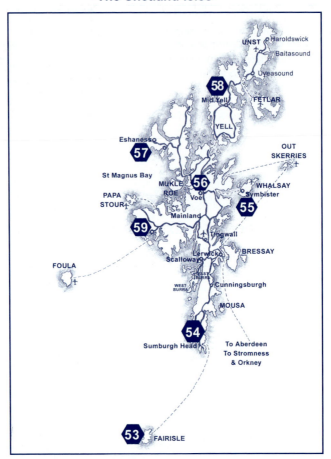

Travel to Shetland

By Air
B.A operate flights to Sumburgh from Aberdeen, Edinburgh, Wick and Inverness.
By Ferry
Northlink Ferries operate a car ferry to Lerwick from Aberdeen, and from Stromness/Scrabster
There are also ferry connections to Norway, Faroes and Iceland.

The Shetland Islands are a group of about 100 islands with only 15 inhabited, 130 miles north of the Scottish mainland. Scenery of the Shetland Islands, beautiful and wild with indented fjord-like, dramatic coastline enclosed by steep hills and bleak windswept inland moors. The mild climate for such a high latitude, 400 miles south of the Arctic Circle, with the waters warmed by the Gulf Stream. Long hours of daylight and sunshine in summer, much lower than average rainfall for the west of Scotland and virtually no midges – but with strong winds at times which has led to a significant lack of trees.
The main town is at Lerwick with many scattered small settlements throughout the smaller islands. Mainland is the largest island here and contains the town of Lerwick. North of Mainland lie the islands of Yell and Unst, and one mile off Unst's coast is the wonderfully named Muckle Flugga lighthouse, the most northerly point of Britain. To the south lies the island of Fair Isle with its stunning bird colonies

The Shetlands were invaded by Norsemen in the 7-8th centuries. They ruled the islands until the 15th century, and many Norse customs still survive. In 1472, the islands with Orkney were annexed to the Scottish Crown but the islands still hold strong links with Scandinavia. Farming on crofts is the mainstay of the economy today with each croft having a few acres of arable land with the right to graze sheep on the 'Scattald' or common grazings. Fishing has always been important, and crofters fish to supplement their diet or their income - the herring-fishing industry, centred on Lerwick, has declined since the mid-20th century and seine fishing for whitefish is now more important. Many men often seek work in the North Sea oil industry or Royal Navy. The discovery of oil in the fields of the North Sea altered Shetland's traditional way of life when the oil terminal and pipelines were built in the 1970's at Sullom Voe. The tankers can be seen approaching as they use the sheltered, deep waters provided by Yell Sound.

Shetland Outdoors
Cycling in the Shetland Islands
The Shetland Islands have 1000 miles of cycling waiting to be explored. Picturesque harbours and fishing boats, lochs, voes and dramatic coastlines alongside the rolling land of the crofting communities.
This is as far north as the UK Cycle Network goes - the top edge of Scotland. Cycling on Shetland can form the first (or last) leg of the 7 country - 6,000 km - signposted North sea Cycle route – followed by the 8 hour boat trip to Orkney for the next leg.
For really interesting cycle rides try these for size:-
On Unst from the Belmont Ferry – OS 1 - 18km route – 2-3 hours -; Whalsay – 11km - 2 hours – circular route to Symbister to Sandwick; Voe –circular route – 36km – 5-6 hours; Mainland Shetland still has old whaling stations with many of the ruined fishing lodges which can be reached by cycle. Eshaness Lighthouse has some of Shetland's most spectacular scenery with blow holes, arches and caves.
The Island of Foula has the 372 metre sheer cliff which is the second highest in Britain - and breathtaking. The isthmus of Mavis Grind where the Atlantic Ocean is only a few meters from the North Sea.
Cycle Hire in Shetland
Granfield Garage	Lerwick	Tel 01595 692709
Sumburgh Hotel	Sumburgh Airport	Tel 01950 460201
Unst	Gardiesauld	Tel 01957 75559

Kayaking in the Shetland Isles
A superb experience to paddle amongst the many islands off the 1450 mile long coastline with skerries, arches, cliffs, caves and stacks. Please be careful – the sea conditions and weather can be very changeable with very strong sea currents for the inexperienced and unprepared. The season usually starts at the end of April. Paddling trips out to Unst, Fetlar, Whalsay, Papa Stour and Bresay are excellent – but need to be well prepared. Shetland Canoe Club welcomes visitors – but contact them well in advance – based at Bridge End Outdoor Centre on Burra.
Kayak Hire in Shetland
Bridge End Outdoor Centre	Burra	Tel 01595 859647

Walking in the Shetland Islands
The longer than usual daylight hours is mid summer – along with the midnight sun – make walking in Shetland a unique experience. Walking routes and tours will have the same back ground as cycling routes – peaceful inland lochs, sandy beaches, heather covered hills and moors with soaring Atlantic and North Sea cliffs – with historic sites, and an array of varied and unique wildlife. You may need headgear to protect yourself from terns and fulmars. Visit the Island of Fetlar – perhaps stay over night – walk goes out to the Bird Reserve – visit standing stones and site of viking boat remains – 14km – fairly easy flat walking; Jarlshof Walk – Mainland Shetland – 6km – visit the famous archeological site and local brochs – passing the Pool of Virkie with migratory wading birds; Mousa Broch Walk – 15 minute boat trip from Hoswick, south of Lerwick – 2 hours – OS 4 – grassy paths and shoreline. Also try the walks on Burra Isle, Whalsay, Unst, Foula, Papa Stoer, St Ninians Isle, Muckle Roe, Outer Skerries.
Events & Festivals
29 January 2004 **Up Helly Aa Fire Festival** – Viking processions by Jarl Squads in Lerwick – torchlit procession and burning of viking Galley.
January – February 2004 **Up Helly Aa Fire Festivals** also in other smaller villages – Nesting and Girlsa, Uyeasound, Northmavine, Bressay, Cullivoe,
Shetland Folk Festival -Shetland Fiddle and Accordian Festival -Walking Festival - Shetland Storytelling Festival

SHETLAND CAMPING BÖD NETWORK

EXPLORE SHETLAND- BED DOWN IN A BÖD!

In Shetland a böd was a building used to house fishermen in season and today the word has been borrowed to describe a network of basic accommodation for those looking for a simple stay in the islands. All the böds are buildings with a historical or cultural significance.

54.Betty Mouat's

Scatness, Sumburgh, Shetland
Sleeps: 8 in bunk beds in 2 common rooms.
Disabled facilities, shower and solid fuel heater.
This böd was once home to the redoubtable Betty Mouat who drifted to Norway alone and lived to tell the tale. Adjacent to the Old Scatness broch archaeological excavation

55.Grieve House

Whalsay, Shetland
Sleeps: 6 in bunk beds in 1 common room.
Solid fuel heater.
NO ELECTRICITY

The great Scottish poet Hugh McDiarmid lived here for 9 years while writing some of his best work.

56.Voe Sail Loft

Voe, Shetland.
Sleeps: 18 in bunk beds in 1 common rooms
Disabled facilities and solid fuel heater.
Once a store for sail fishing boats' gear this largest böd is set in an idyllic setting at the head of a mini fjord.

Fees are £5 per person per night. Exclusive use can be booked.

57. Johnie Notion's

Eshaness, Northmavine, Shetland
Sleeps: 4 in bunk beds in 1 common room.
NO ELECTRICITY
Set amongst some of Shetland's most
spectacular cliff scenery this böd was once
home to smallpox inoculation pioneer John
Williamson known locally as Johnie Notions

58. Windhouse Lodge

Mid Yell, Yell, Shetland.
Sleeps: 12 in bunk beds in 3 common rooms.
Disabled facilities, shower and
solid fuel heater.
The gate house of Shetland's most haunted
ruin this is one of the best equipped böds
and an ideal base for touring the North Isles
of Shetland.

59. Voe House

Walls, Shetland.
Sleeps: 16 in bunk beds in 4 common rooms.
Disabled facilities, shower
and solid fuel heater.
Overlooking the picturesque village of Walls
this böd is a fascinating building carefully
restored using recycled materials. Situated
next to the ruin of a 16th century manse the
kitchen end of the böd was
once a bicycle shop!

Shetland Isles

Scottish Hostels Directory 2003/4

The Hostels and Bunkhouses highlighted in bold below all have full adverts in this guide. The page on which this advert appears is noted alongside the listing. These hostels have all agreed to comply with the agreed operating standards given at the front of this guide. In these hostels you can expect at least these basic minimum standards. You will also find these hostels with area maps on the website
www.scottish-hostels.com
Many of the other hostels and bunkhouses listed in the Scottish Hostels Directory may have been inspected under other grading and inspection schemes elsewhere. Please check at each hostel if you wish to know if a hostel has been inspected.

Those Hostels and bunkhouses denoted "**GB only**" are those which accept Group Bookings only – do not just turn up at these hostels and just expect a bed! The Gatliff Trust Hostels do not have a telephone at the hostel and do not accept pre-bookings – these are denoted "**No PB**". Just turn up at these hostels. At all other hostels – particularly in busy summer high season or the mid winter ski season in some areas – it is always advisable to phone ahead to the hostel of your choice to check for availability.

Name of Hostel	Area / Location	Tel No
GRAMPIAN HIGHLANDS & FIFE		
Glen Clova Steading Bunkhouse	Kirriemuir, Angus	01575 550350
Braemar Lodge	Braemar, Aberdeenshire	013397 41627
St. Andrews Tourist Hostel	St Andrews, Fife	01334 479911
Cairnsmill Bunkhouse	St Andrews, Fife	01334 473604
Rucksacks Braemar (Page 17)	Breamar, Aberdeenshire	01339 741517
Jenny's Bothy Crofthouse	Corgarff, Aberdeenshire	01975 651449
Gulabin Lodge (Page 17)	by Blaigowrie, Glenshee	0777 8941687
Falkland Backpackers	Falkland, Fife	01337 857710
Aberdeen **SYHA**	8 Queen's Road, Aberdeen	0871 330 8503
Inverey **SYHA**	By Braemar, Aberdeenshire	0871 3308526
Braemar **SYHA**	Corrie Feragie, Braemar	0871 3308506
PERTHSHIRE & THE TROSSACHS		
Braveheart Backpackers	Killin, Perthshire	0131 556 5560
Pitlochry Backpackers	Pitlochry,Perthshire	01796 470044
Braincroft Bunkhouse (Page 16)	Comrie, Perthshire	01764 670140
Old Bank House Lodge (Page 16)	Pitlochry, Perthshire	01764 670140
Wester Caputh Independent Hostel	By Dunkeld, Perthshire	01738 710617
Glassie Farm Bunkhouse (Page 16)	Aberfeldy, Perthshire	01887 820265
Dunolly Adventure Outdoors **GB only**	Aberfeldy, Perthshire	01887 820298
Adventurer's Escape	Aberfeldy, Perthshire	01887 820498
Trossachs Backpackers	Callander, Perthshire	01877 331 200
The Willy Wallace Backpackers Hostel	Stirling, Perthshire	01786 446773
Ardoenaig Outdoor Centre Hostel	Loch Tay, Perthshire	01567 820523
Pitlochry **SYHA**	Knockard Road, Pitlochry	0871 3308546
Glendevon **SYHA**	By Dollar, Clackmannanshire	0871 3308523
Killin **SYHA**	Killin, Perthshire	0871 3308532
Stirling **SYHA**	St. John Street, Stirling	0871 3308550
ARGYLL & THE INNER HEBRIDES		
Arle Farm Bunkhouse	Isle of Mull	01680 300343
Lochaline Divers Hostel	Ardnamurchan, Argyll	01967 421301
Iona Bunkhouse	Isle of Iona, Mull, Argyll	01681 700761
Balmeanach Park Bunkhouse	Fishnish, Isle of Mull	01680 300342
Kerrera Bunkhouse	Isle of Kerrera, Oban	01631 570223

Name of Hostel	Area / Location	Tel No
Corran House	Oban, Argyll	01631 566040
Colonsay Backpackers Lodge	Isle of Colonsay	01951 200312
Ardentrive Hostel (Page 33)	Isle of Kerrera, Oban	01631 567180
Oban Backpackers	Oban, Argyll	01631 562107
Jeremy Inglis Hostel	Oban, Argyll	01631 565065
Loch Lomond **SYHA**	Arden, Alexandria, Dumbarton	0871 3308539
Oban **SYHA**	Esplanade, Oban, Argyll	0871 3308545
Rowardennan **SYHA**	By Drymen, Glasgow	0871 3308548
Tobermory **SYHA**	Main Street, Tobermory, Isle of Mull	0871 3308552
Islay **SYHA**	Port Charlotte, Isle of Islay, Argyll	0871 3308528
Crianlarich **SYHA**	Station Road, Crianlarich	0871 3308513
Inveraray **SYHA**	Dalmally Road, Inveraray	0871 3308527
Ardmay House (34)	Loch Lomond, Argyll	01301 702998

STRATHSPEY, BADENOCH & MORAY

Loch Park Adventure Centre	Keith,Moray	01524 810338
Badenoch Christian Centre	Kincraig, Inverness-shire	01540 651373
Ballindalloch Hostel GB (Page 23)	Speyside Way, Moray	01540 651272
Ardenbeg Bunkhouse (23)	Grantown On Spey	01479 872824
Aviemore Independent Bunkhouse	Aviemore, Inverness-shire	01479 811137
Badaguish Outdoor Centre	Aviemore, Inverness-shire	01479 861285
Log Cabin Hostel	Nethy Bridge, Inverness-shire	01479 821331
Nethy Station GB only (Page 24)	Nethy Bridge, Inverness-shire	01479 821370
Nethy House GB only (Page 24)	Nethy Bridge, Inverness-shire	01479 821370
Craigower Lodge	Newtonmore, Inverness-shire	01540 673281
Croftdhu Hostel	Newtonmore, Inverness-shire	01540 673504
Speyside Backpackers (Page 24)	Grantown on Spey, Moray	01479 873514
Fraoch Lodge	Boat of Garten, Inverness-shire	01479 831331
Carrbridge Bunkhouse	Carrbridge, Inverness-shire	01479 841250
Glen Feshie Hostel (Page 25)	Kincraig, Inverness-shire	01540 651323
The Laird's Bothy (Page 25)	Kingussie, Inverness-shire	01540 661334
Aviemore **SYHA**	25 Grampian Road, Aviemore	0871 3308504
Cairngorm Lodge **SYHA**	Glenmore, Aviemore	0871 3308538
Tomintoul **SYHA**	Main Street, Tomintoul, Ballindalloch	0870 1553255
Dulnain Bridge Outdoor (Page 25)	Dulnain BridgeGrantown-On-Spey	01479 851246

INVERNESS & LOCH NESS

Foyers House	Foyers, Loch Ness	
Morag's Lodge (Page 37)	Fort Augustus, Inverness-shire	01320 366289
Invergarry Lodge	Invergarry, Inverness-shire	01809 501412
Loch Ness Backpackers Lodge	Drumnadrochit, Inverness-shire	01456 450807
Pottery Bunkhouse	Laggan,Inverness-shire	01528 544231
The Long Lie In	Inverness	01463 713517
Inverness Student Hostel	Inverness	01463 236556
Ho Ho Hostel	Inverness	01463 221225
Eastgate Backpackers Hostel	Inverness	01463 718756
Bazpackers Backpackers Hostel	Inverness	01463 717663
Cannich **SYHA**	Beauly, Inverness-shire	0871 3308511
Inverness Millburn **SYHA**	Victoria Drive, Inverness City	0871 3308529
Loch Ness **SYHA**	Glenmoriston, Inverness-shire	0871 3308537
Glen Affric **SYHA**	Allt Beith, Glen Affric, Cannich, Beauly	0870 15532355

BEN NEVIS & GLENCOE

Corrour Station Bunkhouse (Page 34)	By Fort William, Inverness-shire	01397 732236
Grey Corrie Lodge	Roybridge, Inverness-shire	01397 712236
Highland Adventure Centre	Knoydart, Loch Nevis	01687 462274

Name of Hostel	Area / Location	Tel No
West Highland Way Sleeper (page 34)	Bridge of Orchy, Argyll	01855 831381
Ben Nevis Bunkhouse	Glen Nevis, By Fort William	01397 701227
Bank Street Lodge (page 36)	Fort William,	01397 700070
Doune Marine Bunkhouse	Knoydart, (mainly GB only)	01687462667
Torrie Shieling	Inverie, Knoydart, Inverness-shire	01687 462764
The Smiddy Bunkhouse (Page 38)	Corpach, Fort William, Inverness-shire	01397 772467
Aite Cruinichidh (Page 37)	Roybridge, Inverness-shire	01397 712315
Glencoe Bunkhouses (Page 35)	Glencoe, Argyll	01855 811256
Blackwater Hostel (Page 36)	Kinlochleven, Argyll	01855 831253
The Inchree Centre (Page 35)	Onich, by Fort William, Inverness-shire	01855 821287
Fort William Backpackers	Fort William, Inverness-shire	01397 700711
Achintee Bunkhouse (Page 36)	Glen Nevis, Fort William	01397 702240
Sheena's Backpackers (Page 38)	Mallaig, Inverness-shire	01687 462764
Glenfinnan Sleeping Car	Glenfinnan, Inverness-shire	01397 722295
Glen Nevis **SYHA**	Glen Nevis, Fort William	0871 3308524
Glencoe **SYHA**	Glencoe, Argyll	0871 3308522
Loch Ossian **SYHA**	Corrour, By Fort William	0871 3308540
Loch Lochy **SYHA**	South Laggan, Inverness-shire	0871 3308536

ISLE OF SKYE & THE SMALL ISLES

Kate's Cottage NTS (Page 48)	Isle of Canna	01687 462466
Kinloch Castle SNH (Page 48)	Isle of Rum	01687 462037
Waterfront Bunkhouse	Carbost, Isle of Skye	01478 640205
Raasay House	Ross-shire	01478 660266
Sligachan Bunkhouse (Page 49)	Isle of Skye	01478 650204
Glen Hinnisdal Bunkhouse	Isle of Skye	01470 552212
Dun Caan Hostel	Kyleakin, Isle of Skye	01599 534 087
The Glebe Barn (Page 47)	Isle of Eigg	01687 482417
Dun Flodigarry Hostel	Uig, Isle of Skye	01470 552212
Portree Independent Hostel	Portree, Isle of Skye	01478 613737
Portree Backpackers Hostel	Portree, Isle of Skye	01478 613641
Skyewalker Hostel (Page 49)	Portnalong, Isle of Skye	0800 0277 059
Croft Bunkhouse & Bothies	Portnalong, Isle of Skye	01478 640254
Flora Macdonald Hostel (Page 48)	Sleat, Isle of Skye	01471 844440
Fossil Bothy Hostel	Isle of Skye. (Tel week day)	01471 822644
Skye Backpackers	Kyleakin, Inverness-shire	01599 534087
Cuchilainn's Hostel	Kyle of Lochalsh, Ross-shire	01599 534492
Kyleakin **SYHA**	Kyleakin, Isle of Skye	0871 3308535
Armadale **SYHA**	Ardvasar, Sleat, Isle of Skye	0871 3308502
Uig **SYHA**	Uig, Isle of Skye	0871 3308556
Broadford **SYHA**	Broadford, Isle of Skye	0871 3308508
Glenbrittle **SYHA**	Glenbrittle, Carbost, Isle of Skye	0871 3308521
Raasay **SYHA**	Creachan Cottage, Raasay, Kyle	0871 3308549

THE WESTERN ISLES

Stornoway Backpackers	Stornoway, Isle of Lewis,	01851 703628
Isle of Barra Hostel	Isle of Barra, Western Isles	01871 810443
Stornoway Surf House (Page 50)	Stornoway, Isle of Lewis	01851 705826
Galson Farm Bunkhouse	South Galston, Isle of Lewis	01851 850492
Drinishader Bunkhouse	By Tarbert, Isle of Lewis	01859 511255
Laxdale Bunkhouse (Page 50)	Laxdale, Isle of Lewis	01851 703234
Rock View Bunkhouse (Page 50)	Tarbert, Isle of Harris	01859 502626
Scaladale Hostel & Centre	Ardvourlie, Isle of Harris	01859 502502

Name of Hostel	Area / Location	Tel No
Am Bothan	Leverburgh, Isle of Harris	01859 520251
Uist Outdoor Centre	Lochmaddy, Isle of N Uist	01876 500480
Taigh Mo Sheanair	Claddach Baleshare, Isle of N Uist	01876 580246
Benbecula Backpackers Hostel	Balivanich, Isle of Benbecula	01870 602706
Berneray - *Hebridean Hostels Trust*	Isle of Berneray, North Uist (No PB)	ghht@gatliff.org.uk
Garenin - *Hebridean Hostels Trust*	Carloway, Isle of Lewis (No PB)	ghht@gatliff.org.uk
Howmore - *Hebridean Hostels Trust*	South Uist (No PB)	ghht@gatliff.org.uk
Rhenigidale - *Hebridean Hostels Trust*	Rhenigidale, Isle of Harris (No PB)	ghht@gatliff.org.uk
Kershader – Commumity Hostel	Kershader, South Lochs, Isle of Lewis	01851 880236

ROSS-SHIRE & THE NW COAST

Wee Bunkhouse	Glen Sheil, Ross-shire	01599 511275
Glen Affric Backpackers	Glen Affric, Inverness-shire	01456 415236
Badrallach Bothy (Page 57)	Dundonnel, Wester Ross	01854 6332810
Talladale Bothie	Torridon, Wester Ross	01445 760288
Mol Mor NTS (Page 56)	Torridon, Wester Ross	0131 243 9331
Tigh Iseabeal (Page 54)	Nr Kyle, Ross-shire	01599 588205
Silver Fir Bunkhouse (54)	Dornie, Wester Ross	01599 555 264
Plocton Station Bunkhouse	Plocton, Ross-shire	01599 544235
Achnashellach Hostel (Page 55)	Strathconon, Wester Ross	01520 766232
Morvich, Kintail NTS (Page 55)	Kintail, Wester Ross	0131 243 9331
Blackrock Bunkhouse	Evanton, Ross-shire	01349 830917
Strathconnon Inn Cabin	Dalnacruich, Ross-shire	01997 477201
Rua Reidh Lighthouse (Page 56)	Gairloch, Ross-shire	01445 771263
Kinlochewe Bunkhouse	Kinlochewe, Wester Ross	01445 760254
Sail Mhor Croft Hostel (Page 57)	Dundonnel, Ross-shire	01854 633224
West House (Page 57)	Ullapool, Ross-shire	01854 613126
Cougie Lodge (page 55)	Strathglas, Beauly, Inverness-shire	01456 415459
Torridon **SYHA**	Shieldaig, Ross-shire	0871 3308553
Strathpeffer **SYHA**	Strathpeffer, Ross-shire	0871 3308564
Carn Dearg **SYHA**	Gairloch, Ross-shire	0871 3308510
Achininver **SYHA**	Achiltibuie, Ullapool, Ross-shire	0871 3308501
Craig **SYHA**	Diabaig, Achnasheen, Ross-Shire	0870 1553255
Ullapool **SYHA**	Shore Street, Ullapool	0871 3308555
Ratagan **SYHA**	Glenshiel, Kyle, Ross-shire	0871 3308547

SUTHERLAND & CAITHNESS

Kylesku Lodges	Ullapool, Sutherland	01971 502003
Lazy Crofter Bunkhouse (Page 63)	Durness, Sutherland	01971 511209
Inchnadamph Lodge (Page 62)	Assynt, Sutherland	01571 822232
Thurso Youth Club (Page 63)	Thurso, Caithness	01847 892964
Sandra's Backpackers (Page 64)	Thurso, Caithness	01847 894575
sleeperzzz.com (Page 63)	Rogart, Sutherland	01408 641343
Carbisdale Castle **SYHA**	Culrain, Sutherland	0871 3308509
Durness **SYHA**	Smoo, Lairg	0871 3308514
Helmsdale **SYHA**	Helmsdale, Sutherland	0871 3308525
Tongue **SYHA**	Tongue, By Lairg, Sutherland	0871 3308554
John O' Groats **SYHA**	Canisbay, Near Wick, Caithness	0871 3308530
Achmelvich **SYHA**	Recharn, Lairg, Sutherland	0871 3308505

ORKNEY ISLANDS

Bisgoes Hostel (Page 69)	Papa Westray, Orkney	01857 677420
Peedie Hostel (Page 69)	Kirkwall, Mainland Orkney	01856 875477
St Margaret's Hope Backpackers	South Ronaldsay, Orkney	01856 831205

Name of Hostel	Area / Location	Tel No
Stronsay Fishmart Hostel	Stronsay, Orkney	01857 616213
Observatory Hostel RSPB	North Ronaldsay, Orkney	01857 633200
Birsay Hostel	Birsay, Orkney	01856 873535
The Barn	Westray, Orkney	01857 677214
Rousay Hostel	Rousay, Orkney	01856 821252
Wheems Bothy (Organic Farm)	South Ronaldsay, Orkney	01856 831535
Browns Hostel	Stromness, Orkney	01856 850661
Kirkwall **SYHA**	Old Scapa Road, Kirkwall, Orkney	08713 308533
Stromness **SYHA**	Hellihole Road, Stromness, Orkney	08713 308551
Hoy **SYHA**	Hoy, Stromness, Orkney	01856 873535
Rackwick **SYHA**	Hoy, Stromness, Orkney	01856 873535
Eday **SYHA**	London Bay, Eday, Orkney	01857 622206
Papa Westray **SYHA**	Beltane house, Papa Westray, Orkney	01857 644267

SHETLAND & FAIR ISLE

Gardiesfauld Hostel	Isle of Unst, Shetland Isles	01957 755259
Windhouse Lodge – BöD (Page 73)	Mid Yell, Isle of Yell	01595 693434
Grieve House – BöD (Page72)	Isle of Whalsay	01595 693434
Sail Loft – BöD (Page 72)	Voe,Delting, North Mainland	01595 693434
Betty Mouats – BöD (Page 72)	Dunrossness, South Mainland	01595 693434
Voe House – BöD (Page73)	Walls, West Mainland	01595 693434
Johnnie Notions – BöD (Page 73)	Hamnavoe, North Mainland	01595 693434
Puffin Hostel NTS (Page 69)	Fair Isle	01463 232034
Cunningsburgh Village Club	Cunningsburgh, South Mainland	01950 477241
Lerwick **SYHA**	King Harald Street, Lerwick	01595 692114

DUMFRIES, GALLOWAY, AYRSHIRE

Stranraer Hostel	Dumfries & Galloway	01776 703395
Well Road Centre Hostel	Dumfries & Galloway	01683 221040
Shore Lodge Bunkhouse	Lothian	0131 2439331
Barnsoul Farm Hostel	Dumfries	01387 730294 or 703453
Marthrown of Marble	Dumfries	01387 247900
Sally's Hoose	Stranraer, Wigtonshire	01776 703395
Galloway Lodge	Castle Douglas	01644 420626
Biscayne House	Largs, Ayrshire	01475 672851
Aldersyde Bunkhouse	Isle of Arran	01770 600959
High Corrie Croft	Isle of Arran	01770 302303
Kendoon **SYHA**	Dalry, Castle Douglas	0871 3308531
Minnigaff **SYHA**	Newton Stewart, Wigtownshire	0871 3308542
Wanlockhead **SYHA**	Wanlockhead, Lanarkshire	0871 3308557
Lochranza **SYHA**	Lochranza, Isle of Arran	0871 3308541
Whiting Bay **SYHA**	Whiting Bay, Isle of Arran	0871 3308558

STRATHCLYE & GLASGOW

Glades House Hostel	Strathclyde	0141 639 2601
Cairncross House	Strathclyde	0141 221 9334
Strathclyde University Campus	Strathclyde	0141 553 4148
Glasgow Backpackers Hostel	Glasgow, Strathclyde	0141 3329099
Bunkum Backpackers	Glasgow, Strathclyde	0141 5814481
Glasgow **SYHA**	8 Park Terrace, Glasgow	08701 55 32 55
New Lanark **SYHA**	Rosedale Street, New Lanark	0871 3308544

Name of Hostel	Area / Location	Tel No
LOTHIANS & EDINBURGH		
Highlander Backpackers	Edinburgh, Lothian	0800 073 0558
St Christopher's Inn Hostel	Edinburgh, Lothian	0131 226 1446
Budget Backpackers Hostel	Edinburgh, Lothian	0131 226 6351
Brodies Backpackers (Page 79)	Edinburgh, Lothian	0131 556 6770
Belford Hostel	Edinburgh, Lothian	0131 225 6209
Argyl Backpackers Hostel	Edinburgh, Lothian	0131 667 9991
Caledonian Backpackers	Edinburgh, Lothian	0131 476 7224
Royal Mile High Street Backpackers	Edinburgh, Lothian	
Princess Street West Backers Hostel	Edinburgh, Lothian	0131 2262939
BlackFriars High Street Hostel	Edinburgh, Lothian	0131 5573984
Edinburgh Backpackers Hostel	Edinburgh, Lothian	0131 220 2200
Cowgate Hostel	Edinburgh, Lothian	0131 226 2153
Castle Rock Hostel	Edinburgh, Lothian	0131 225 9666
Laetare International Centre	Linlithgow, West Lothian	01506 842214
Edinburgh Bruntsfield **SYHA**	Bruntsfield, Edinburgh	0871 3308515
Edinburgh Central **SYHA**	Cowgate, Edinburgh	0871 3308517
Edinburgh Eglinton **SYHA**	Eglinton Crescent, Edinburgh	0871 3308516
Edinburgh International **SYHA**	Guthrie Street, Edinburgh	0871 3308519
Edinburgh Pleasance **SYHA**	Pleasance, Edinburgh	0871 3308518
SCOTTISH BORDERS		
Broadmeadows **SYHA**	Yarrowford, Selkirk	0871 3308507
Kirk Yetholm **SYHA**	Kelso, Roxburghshire	0871 3308534
Melrose **SYHA**	Priorwood, Melrose, Roxburghshire	0871 3308543
Coldingham Sands **SYHA**	Coldingham Sands, Coldingham,	0871 3308512

As far as we are aware all the details given here are correct at the time of going to print.
Please let us know if any telephone numbers are incorrect, if there is any hostel not included - or even if hostels have closed down.
In the unlikely event that you should experience a problem with any hostel listed here

please contact us on
guide@scottish-hostels.com or
Tel / Fax No 01397 772411.

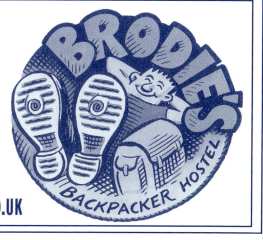

Hostel Directory

Website Directory:

www.scottish-hostels.com - details on all the Hostels in this guide, plus travel & activity information & many links.

The main Tourist Board websites are worth a visit – such as:

www.visitscotland.com	Pan Scotland Information
www.highlandfreedom.com	Highlands Tourist Board
www.walkingwild.com	Scottish Walking Site
www.escapetotheedge.co.uk	Around the Coast & Islands
www.wannabethere.com	Action breaks
www.visitorkney.com	Orkney Tourist Board
www.visitshetland.com	Shetland Tourist Board
www.visithebrides.com	Western Isles Tourist Board
www.perthshire.co.uk	Perthshire Tourist Board
www.castlesandwhisky.com	Aberdeen & Grampian TB

Independent Guides to Scotland may offer a more informal view of Scotland & the Highlands – try:

www.scotland-info.co.uk - 'The Internet Guide to Scotland' or
www.undiscoveredscotland.co.uk which covers the Highlands in quite some detail, and has links to many local sites.

Scottish Hostels Vouchers

Below are four 50p vouchers.
These can be used in participating hostels
for a 50p discount on your second night's stay

Only one voucher per person at any one time may be used.
Just present your guide to the participating hostels
(marked with 'V') only
and your voucher will be crossed
and the 50p reduction will be given